*Please Leave Your Shoes
at the Door*

To my friend Marilyn Glenn,

"For whether we live, we live unto the
Lord; and whether we die, we die
unto the Lord: whether we live or
die, we are the Lord's. For this end
Christ both died, and rose, and revived,
that He might be Lord both of the dead
and the living" Romans 14:8-9

"Therefore if any man be in Christ, he
is a new creature: old things are
passed away; behold all things are
become new. And all things are of
God, who has reconciled us to
himself and given us the ministry
of reconciliation" 2 Corinthians 5:17-18

Becky Phillips

PLEASE LEAVE YOUR SHOES AT THE DOOR

THE STORY OF
ELMER AND CORRINE SAHLBERG

Corrine Sahlberg

Christian Publications

CAMP HILL, PENNSYLVANIA

Christian Publications
3825 Hartzdale Drive, Camp Hill, PA 17011

The mark of ✝ *vibrant faith*

ISBN: 0-87509-486-4
LOC Catalog Card Number: 91-77848
© 1992 by Christian Publications
All rights reserved
Printed in the United States of America

92 93 94 95 96   5 4 3 2 1

Cover photo illustration
© 1992, Karl Foster

SOUTHEAST ASIA

China

VIETNAM

Hanoi ★

LAOS

Xiangkhoang ●

Myanmar

South China Sea

Vientiane ★
● Nongkhai

THAILAND

● Udorn

Khon Kaen ●

Bangkok ★

KAMPUCHEA

Andaman Sea

● Dalat

Phnom Penh ★

Ho Chi Minh City ●

Gulf of Siam

Malay Peninsula

Sumatra

Penang ●

Malaysia

● Tanah Rata

Contents

Acknowledgments 1

Foreword 2

Preface 4

1 Choices 11

2 Six Reasons Why I Shouldn't
Be a Missionary 19

3 The Terrible Tones 24

4 Shots out of the Darkness 31

5 Widow with a Husband 42

6 Golden Temples and Yellow Robes 56

7 Little MKs 63

8 Goodbyes at Bangkok Airport 70

9 The School That Kept Moving 82

10 I Am Going to Kill You 95

*11 Snake in the Grass
(and in the Bedroom) 103*

*12 From the Farm Field
to the Mission Field 110*

13 Please Don't Let My Daddy Die 114

14 Dr. Jesus 121

15 In the Middle of a Revolution 128

16 On the Road Again 136

17 Dumb like a Buffalo 146

18 Hold Up Your Fingers 151

19 Just Eat—Don't Ask 159

20 I Gave You to God 165

21 A Seed Is Sown 169

22 We're the Team 175

Epilogue 191

Acknowledgments

I want to thank my son, Dale, for spending many hours typing this manuscript. I appreciate his suggestions, his constructive criticism and his valuable help in so many ways.

I also want to express thanks to my husband, Elmer, for his advice, encouragement and patience during the process of writing this book.

Foreword

This book is the story of a dedicated, determined missionary couple who spent a lifetime winning people to Jesus Christ and discipling them into reproducing Christians.

I first became acquainted with the Sahlbergs just before they left for Thailand. Then, on several furloughs, our paths of ministry crossed. On one furlough, they attended the church that I pastored and I had the privilege of baptizing their oldest daughter.

After graduation from Nyack College, Elmer and Corrine served in a pastorate in Prattville, Alabama, just outside of Montgomery, on the road to Selma. When they arrived, these two Northerners found a small struggling church. By the time they left, every home in Prattville had been visited and a good foundation laid for the future growth of that church. All of Prattville, it seemed, loved the Sahlbergs.

In this book you will gain insight into the struggles, heartaches, loneliness, joy and victories of daily missionary life as graphically portrayed by a missionary wife and mother. And you will catch a glimpse of the culture of the gentle, beautiful Thai people and their land.

Probably the most intriguing part of this account is the dogged determination that is so clearly revealed. Dogged determination enabled Corrine Sahlberg to overcome many obstacles when God called her to serve Him in Thailand.

Dogged determination allowed her to learn a most difficult tonal language. Dogged determination enabled the Sahlbergs to live in the home of Paul and Priscilla Johnson, a young missionary couple cruelly martyred as they held a church service. It was dogged determination coupled with evident love for God and for the Thai people that carried them through even the most difficult circumstances.

It is with real pleasure that I commend *Please Leave Your Shoes at the Door* to you.

Paul Alford
President, Toccoa Falls College
Toccoa Falls, Georgia
September 3, 1991

Preface

Dear Mom,

We were gone all week up in the mountains of northeast Thailand. I didn't see a chair, a bed or a bathroom the whole time. We sat on the floor, slept on the floor and ate on the floor. Elmer seems quite adept at those things, but it is hard for me. There were some benches to sit on in the meeting places, but they were very rough and uncomfortable. We ate Thai food with the Thai Christians. It has been extremely hot, even at night.

When Elmer and I arrived in Thailand in 1950 as new missionaries, it was evident that our lifestyle was going to have to change drastically to fit in with the local culture and customs. We soon found out that such upheaval could be most unsettling. We learned that a whole set of social patterns could not be either denied or learned overnight.

To assist in the aculturation process, our Mission, The Christian and Missionary Alliance, produced a sheaf of typed pages entitled "Orientation Notes." Their purpose was to help us to become socially acceptable in this new culture and to avoid offending the citizens of our adopted country.

Western customs, the notes said, were accepted in the larger cities but not in the small towns and villages. We should therefore learn to be adaptable. They further warned: "You will find the pace of life and general outlook considerably different. As a whole, the Thai people are fatalists and possess a general apathy about their spiritual, mental, and physical condition."

We soon found out that the "general outlook considerably different" stems from the way Thai people show respect for the head. For instance, a Thai adult would be very offended if someone touched his or her head. Thais believe that the head, being the highest part of the body, should be respected. One must never reach over a person's head without first receiving permission to do so. Even when getting suitcases down from a luggage rack on the train, the rule must be followed.

Neither does one walk near a person's head when he or she is resting on a mat on the floor, nor pass in front of people, either sitting or standing, without excusing oneself and respectfully lowering the head.

Even with the orientation notes to guide us, we often did not understand (or remember) what was proper and expected of us. There were rules for dress, for eating, for gift giving, for receiving guests, for attending weddings and funerals.

Rules. Rules. Rules.

Thailand's most important customs concerned respect for the Buddhist religion and its images. We learned that "all Buddha images—

large or small, ruined or not—are sacred objects which must be respected." This did not mean that we were to take part in Buddhist ceremonies. However, we did not speak against anything connected with Buddha. That would be grounds, we were warned, for an escorted trip to the airport!

Great respect must also be shown towards the king and queen and all members of the royal family. The king is above comparison with anyone, even in a complimentary way. Thailand's king and queen are greatly loved because of their willingness to mix with the populace and their dedication to a variety of special projects.

The law even states that names such as "King," "Queenie," "Prince" or "Princess" must never be given to a dog. Dogs are considered the lowest of all animals. One rebellious man named his dog "King" and received a three-month jail sentence!

In spite of the detailed orientation notes, on one occasion, I unknowingly broke a cultural rule. Our family had planned a trip on a river launch on the Mekong River. The launch was waiting at the edge of the wooden pier when we arrived. Elmer, carrying two-year-old David, jumped on the boat and took a seat near the back. I hopped over the side and noticed an empty seat near the front.

Trying to keep my balance, I hurriedly sat down on the seat.

Suddenly there was dead silence! Glares

replaced smiles. I had obviously done something wrong, but what, I didn't know. At that moment, a yellow-robed Buddhist priest jumped up from the seat next to me and strode angrily to the bow of the boat. Only later did I remember what the notes had advised: "A woman must never sit next to a Buddhist priest."

Some months later, I unwittingly broke another rule while I was helping to sell some household articles of a former missionary. The items were displayed on tables and racks and on the floor. When a Thai lady asked about a certain item, I pointed my foot in the direction of the article on the floor.

"You must never, never point with your foot," a Thai man scolded. That rule was also in the notes: "The feet are thought to be lowly objects. You must not point them at anyone or anything."

Other cultural mores governed the display of affection between men and women. The Thai do not like public physical contact with the opposite sex. They do not show affection in public. Our orientation notes stated, "Missionary couples should avoid public displays of affection."

In this matter of physical contact, we found out that the Thai Christians were offended by the way missionaries conducted baptismal services. One of the Thai leaders told Elmer, "We do not like the way you foreigners hold our women in your arms in the baptismal service."

The correct way to baptize, they said, was to gently push on the head, after receiving permission, of course, and then on the shoulders. The missionaries adapted their baptismal procedures to conform to local custom.

I do not wish to say that all cultural differences were uncomfortable or problematical for us. On the contrary, some local customs are quite delightful. When the Thai greet each other, they put the palms of their hands together graciously, the elbows next to the body and fingers close together and straight. Then they raise their palms up and bend the head at the same time. The more respect one has for the person he meets, the lower he bends his head. It is a beautiful gesture that expresses most eloquently the gentleness of the Thai people.

Elmer adapted easily to the Thai custom of no coats and ties. Under the heading "New Official Government Dress," dated June 29, 1980, the English newspaper in Bangkok announced the official uniform. "The Thai Identity Committee chaired by General Sermna Nakhon," it said, "has decided to make the costume designed by His Majesty the King the official government uniform."

The costume was a special shirt, made of Thai silk or fine handwoven cotton, which would be worn with regular trousers. A long-sleeved shirt would be worn for official occasions and short-sleeved shirts were appropriate at other times. These shirts were never tucked in, so sashes of any color could be added. A "black tie" affair would dictate a black sash added to a white silk shirt.

Another custom having to do with dress code was that shoes must not be worn in Thai homes or temples. Signs saying, "Please leave your shoes at the door" are posted at the entrances to all Buddhist temples and a temple guard or policeman is there to enforce the rule. Our notes stated, "Removal of shoes is not necessarily a sign of respect to the image in the temple. If you are reluctant to take off your shoes, don't go in at all."

In larger temples, special shoe racks are provided. Each person receives a numbered ticket and places his or her shoes in the corresponding box in the rack.

The shoe custom applies to Thai homes as well. At the door of most Thai dwellings one will see shoes lined up. The notes stated, "Shoes are to be removed before entering a Thai home, even if your host tells you not to do so. Tramping on the floor with shoes on is the same as tramping on someone's bed with shoes."

Leaving one's shoes at the door is one of the customs that remained with us as we retired in America after 35 years of missionary service in Thailand. You'll see a sign at our home in Florida which says, "Please leave your shoes at the door."

Let me personalize the invitation to you, my

readers. Please take off your shoes and come on in and have a chair while I share with you how God helped me as a missionary wife and mother to cope with the problems and to share in the rewards of serving God in a foreign land.

Every 10 days for over 30 years, Corrine Sahlberg wrote her mother. Mrs. Henricksen saved all the letters. It is from those letters, Mrs. Sahlberg's own diary, general newsletters, *Alliance Life* articles and copies of *The Task*, the Thailand Mission magazine, that the details of this book were gleaned. Individual chapters are presented topically rather than chronologically.

1

Choices

Dear Mom,

   Last week we went in the Land Rover to visit a group of Cambodian Christians near the Thailand/Cambodia border. We parked the vehicle on the main road and walked about a mile, often through mud and water up to our knees, to the meeting place. Boiling hot sun!

The men walked ahead of me. Not only is that Thai custom—I couldn't keep up with them. My rubber sandals kept sliding in the mud. I wished I had remembered to bring an umbrella or hat to keep off the tropical sun.

Carefully I lifted one foot in front of the other, always on the lookout for a snake or a hole camouflaged in the dirty brown water.

The meeting place, a farmer's home, was surrounded by flooded rice fields partitioned by narrow dirt dikes. I did not relish trying to maneuver those slippery dikes. I wanted to turn back.

Determined to persevere, however, I tucked

up my long Thai skirt between my legs and climbed up on one of the dikes. Suddenly a thought struck me: *What a strange place for a middle-aged American woman to be! I could be in a lovely Florida home enjoying the luxuries of American life. I could be with our four children there. What in the world am I doing here?*

Even as those thoughts swirled in my mind, I knew without a doubt what I was doing there. I had *chosen* to be there. I *wanted* to be a missionary. I *wanted* to go wherever the Lord led me. I was happy. I was doing God's will.

Apparently, I had always wanted to be a missionary. My mother told me that when I was just four years old, I put on my aunt's Salvation Army bonnet and said, "I'm going to be a preacher like Aunt Cora."

Even at that early age, I made a *choice*. That choice was the first of many that set my life on a path that would eventually take me to a land halfway around the world.

At six years of age I made another *choice*—the most important *choice* of all—to invite Jesus into my heart.

Aunt Cora had taken me to a children's meeting in New York City. I will never forget the old man with the white beard who spoke at the service. Years later, I found a book written about this man—Commissioner Samuel Brengle of the Salvation Army. He had a special way of reaching children, the book said, and many children were converted in his meetings. I attended one of those meetings and I was one of those children.

Another *choice* was made some years later, this time not by me, but by my mother. A stranger stopped by our home.

"My name is Mrs. Clingen," she said, "and I belong to The Christian and Missionary Alliance Church. I saw all the children playing outside and I want to invite you and them to our Sunday school and church."

"I don't have time to go to church," my mother explained. "My eight children take all my time."

But Mrs. Clingen persisted, promising that someone from the church would pick up the older children every Sunday if my mother would give permission for them to attend. For years someone did come to pick us up every Sunday. I believe now that except for the dedication and faithfulness of those people I might never have become a missionary.

The annual missionary conference in that church made a great impression on me. Two of the local young people were already in Bible school preparing for missionary service. I wanted to be like them.

My desire to be a missionary like them spawned another *choice*. At age 13, I knelt at the altar in the church and gave my life to God to serve Him in any foreign land. Strangely, no one came to pray with me, but God was there. He placed His hand on me that day and I knew it.

There was a quiet assurance in my heart that God wanted me to be a missionary.

In my late teens, the attractions of the world began to crowd out God's voice. One day my mother said something to me about going to Bible school. As far as she knew that would have been a logical response toward my goal of being a missionary. My answer was not what she expected.

"I am never going to Bible school!" I retorted. "I'll never be a missionary!"

The next summer, however, I was at summer camp and God spoke to me once more through a challenging missionary message. Later that night, during evening devotions, the girls in the dormitory knelt in prayer and then sang, "Where He Leads Me, I Will Follow." I was not of the same mind. Not only was I thinking "no," but I actually said it out loud. I was very embarrassed by the outburst and rushed outside to the shelter of the shadowy porch.

The camp director's wife followed me. She and her husband, Jack Wyrtzen, pled with me to surrender my life for service to God. I was not willing to do that. Mr. Wyrtzen then asked me a strange question, "Are you willing to be made willing?"

I thought for a moment and then decided that to that question I could answer "yes." In the quiet summer night, Jack Wyrtzen prayed that God would make me willing to follow Him.

Back home, nothing changed. I was 20 years old. I was making big money in an airplane factory. World War II was raging in the Pacific. Planes were in great demand. Never had I made so much money. *Finally*, I thought, *I will be able to buy pretty clothes and enjoy life.*

But God was not finished with me. One memorable night I came home from work and went into the bedroom to change clothes. I flipped on the radio beside my bed, and as I did so a voice boomed out, "What are you doing with your life?"

The question startled me. It was like the voice of God to my heart. I turned the radio off and knelt beside my bed. It was time to make another *choice*. I decided that evening to quit my job and go to Bible school.

The very next day I went to the foreman's office to give my notice.

"I was just going to give you a promotion," he said when he heard the news. "Don't leave now. You can earn more money and go later."

"But I must go to Bible college this year," I replied. "This is the *choice* I am making."

In 1943, the Missionary Training Institute (now called Nyack College) offered a special one-year course for students who had not finished high school. I applied to take the course and the college studies that would follow. Soon a letter came from President Thomas Mosely saying that I was accepted for the fall semester.

There was very little time to prepare for

school and very little money in the bank. My mother offered to help me the first year and from then on I worked my way through—doing housework in local homes, helping in the college dining room and working part-time in a paper factory. I was happy. I knew that I had made the right *choice!*

It was at the Missionary Training Institute that Elmer and I met. In the spring of 1946, a group of 13 recently discharged GIs came to study at the Institute. These men, just back from the battlefields of World War II, felt God's call to fulltime ministry. Elmer was part of that group.

At the college, students were given assigned seats in the dining room. On Friday nights, however, we were allowed to sit wherever we wished. The first Friday night of the new semester, one of the soldiers came to the table where my two roommates and I were sitting along with several others. As the group introduced themselves, I noticed that the name Sahlberg sounded like a Swedish name. Since I am of Norwegian background, I struck up a conversation with Elmer and we chatted about our Scandinavian heritage.

During that next year, Elmer and I became good friends. We often talked together, played Ping-Pong and ice skated at a downtown pond. But there were no dates. There was good reason for that on both sides. He told me that he planned to go to New Guinea (now Irian Jaya) as a single missionary. He considered the country too dangerous for a woman. I told him that I too planned to go to the mission field alone.

However, two months before I was to graduate from college, Elmer asked me to go to a basketball game in downtown Nyack. That became the first of many dates. It wasn't long until we knew that we were God's *choice* for each other.

Just before I graduated, Elmer and I were engaged. While he completed his last year, I took a one-year practical nursing course at Booth Memorial Hospital in New York City. We were married in Long Island, New York, in the fall of 1948.

Our two years of required home service were spent in Prattville, Alabama. While we were there, Elmer received news of our appointment. I remember the occasion as if it were yesterday. I was at my mother's home in Florida recuperating from an illness and I was outside hanging baby clothes on the line when my mother called, "There's a telegram here for you."

The telegram was from Elmer. It stated: "Headquarters asks: Will you accept appointment to Siam? Must know immediately. Told them we are willing."

Siam! What a surprise! That area of the world had hardly even been mentioned at the Institute. All I could think of was Siamese cats, Siamese twins and *Anna and the King of Siam!* Elmer's heart had been set on going to New Guinea. He later told me that he was disappointed that we had been asked to go to Siam. But God spoke to him from a devotional reading: "It matters not what happens to your will, but it does matter greatly what happens to God's will."

Siam, we believed, was God's will—God's *choice*.

It was our *choice*, too!

2

Six Reasons Why I Shouldn't Be a Missionary

Dear Mom,
How thankful I am for all your love and the thousands of prayers. A lot of letters have gone between us over these years. God has been so good to me.

Although my mother had always wanted me to be a missionary, there were at least six "good" reasons why I shouldn't have made it to the mission field. One fellow missionary, who had known me as a teenager, said, "Corrine, it just amazes me that you, of all the young people in that church on Long Island, should be out here as a missionary!"

During a furlough, after I had finished speaking in a women's meeting, a former pastor's wife in the Long Island church said to me, "Corrine, I just can't believe that you've really made it to the mission field!"

I knew what both of them meant. There were a number of factors that made me a most unlikely candidate for missionary service.

I had not come from a good home environment. I can remember a time when my father served God. Then, "just one little drink" became one more, until alcohol controlled him. My mother, a devout Christian, did her best to keep our family together, but with eight small children, she seldom had time to go to church. That one of those children would become a missionary was highly unlikely except for God's intervention. And intervene He did, in a most unusual way.

There was also a shortage of money. Because of his drinking problem, my father lost job after job. What money he did make went for liquor. The situation deteriorated until our family was eventually forced to go on welfare. Relatives and other agencies helped us as well. My aunt brought used clothes from my cousins and the Salvation Army provided food baskets at Thanksgiving and Christmas. All of our toys came from the Salvation Army. But God had something special in mind for one of those poor little children. I could never have imagined all that His plan would include.

And then there was my education—or should I say, lack of education. I liked school. But one day my father said, "Corrine, you are 16 years old now. It is time to quit school and get a job and help bring in some money." I remember crying, but I had no choice but to quit.

Besides all those reasons, *I had no obvious talents.* I had no musical ability. I had not learned to play an instrument. I could hardly carry a tune. Worst of all, I found it very difficult to speak in front of an audience. A teacher once told me, "You'll never be a public speaker." I believed her.

A fifth reason why I should never have become a missionary was that *I had no time to participate in church functions.* I had never become involved in the ministry of the church. I only attended the services. Besides, I was shy and quiet and felt left out and inferior because of the reputation of my alcoholic father.

And, lastly, *the weight of family responsibility rested heavily on me.* I felt, rightly or wrongly, that I was my mother's "right hand" because of the way my father drank. She and my younger brothers and sisters needed not only my help, but my financial assistance as well. In fact, I pictured myself helping to provide for the family for the rest of my life.

But God, step by step, miraculously overruled in the difficulties I thought impossible to overcome.

As a young man, my father had been a sailor. When the U.S. government enlisted experienced seamen to help in the World War II lend-lease program, he returned to the sea with the merchant marines. On his first trip back from

Russia to the United States, a German submarine torpedoed his ship. Thirteen men lost their lives. My father was one of them.

In a strange way this event helped start a new life for me, for my father had taken out life insurance. That money, along with the monthly allowances for the younger children, made it possible for my mother to provide for the family and freed me from the responsibility.

My mother was delighted with my decision to go to Bible school. She decided to tithe money from her income to send me. "If you don't take this money," she said, "I'll give it to someone else." I accepted her offer and off I went.

With some of the major stumbling blocks taken care of by God, only the matter of public speaking remained a seemingly insurmountable challenge. It wasn't until I became a missionary that I was finally able to speak before large groups of people. I had read somewhere that "you can't be both self-conscious and God-conscious." I decided not to be self-conscious and made a choice to be God-conscious. God needed my voice to tell the Thai people about Jesus Christ, and He needed my voice to acquaint the people in North America with the needs of the Thai people. Now I actually enjoy speaking and with each new assignment, I remember that I am God's voice for that occasion.

My six "good" reasons for not being able to go to the mission field were not important to

God. What people thought was not important to God either. God had a plan for my life. He wanted me to be a missionary.

With His help, I became His missionary.

3

The Terrible Tones

Dear Mom,

Hello there. It's hard to imagine us way off in Siam, isn't it? But here we are! We started to study the Siamese language the third day after we arrived—five tones, forty-four consonants and thirty-two vowels! We have already learned the alphabet and can say many words.

David causes quite a stir because of his white skin and blonde hair. Crowds of children follow us when we go shopping. There are only eleven white people in this entire area, all Christian and Missionary Alliance missionaries.

We were in Thailand only a few days when we were informed that language study would begin immediately. We had assumed that language study would be a priority, so we were not surprised by the news. We were also informed that a Thai girl would be hired to look after our baby. That was a shock! We had not realized that the Mission rules required us to have a babysitter take care of our 14-month-old David for the six hours of each day that we would spend in study. But rules were rules.

The girl did not know a word of English and had never taken care of an American child. This was not going to be easy. It would take a little ingenuity to make the plan work. I wrote out two pages of instructions and the Mission chairman wrote the Thai translation next to my English sentences. When I wanted something done, I would point to the Thai sentence and she would know what to do.

Also, within days of our arrival, we received a letter of welcome (and instructions) from one of our fellow missionaries.

"As the language examiner," he wrote, "I take pleasure in presenting to you the *Course of Study of the Siamese Language*. You are very fortunate in having excellent teachers and we trust you make rapid progress in the language. Your teachers know English but are instructed to use it as little as possible in order that you may make rapid progress in Siamese."

Thus began our two-year, six-hour-a-day language study program. Unfortunately, it soon became evident that I would never make the "rapid progress" the examiner hoped for. Rather, language study for me became the time of the terrible tones! I remember asking my mother to have the people in the church pray for me because I seemed to be tone deaf, a rather serious situation when trying to learn a tonal language! They thought I said "stone deaf" and were praying for my healing!

I had always hoped that God would call me to a country where the language was not tonal. Instead, I found myself learning a language that has five tones (levels or pitches). A slight mistake in tone can completely change the meaning of a word.

One Thai word, pronounced "kow," means many different things according to the tone one uses and the way it is drawn out or cut off. It can mean rice, to enter a room, the horn of a buffalo, your house, the color white, news, he, she or they! Another thing makes the written language even more difficult—there are no capital letters, no punctuation marks and the breaks between words are at the writer's discretion!

After three months of language study, I was ready to pack my suitcase and head back to America. I couldn't keep up with the others in the class and to make matters worse, the Thais would ask, "Why don't you speak the language like your husband does?" That was not a question that a person in my position wanted to hear. I was utterly discouraged.

One day, about at the end of my rope, I went into a room alone to pray. I poured out my heart to God—the discouragement, the frustration, the futility of it all. As I prayed and agonized before the Lord it seemed that a light bulb flashed on inside my head. In that moment, God gave me the assurance that He would help me learn the language. The terrible (tone) burden lifted and I began to comprehend in a new way.

In addition to the already difficult process, our language study was interrupted by the tragic murder of our dear missionary friends, Paul and Priscilla Johnson. (More on this in the next chapter.) We had just moved to a newly rented house up on the Mekong River, but after their death, the Mission asked us to move once again, this time to live temporarily in the Johnsons' home.

On top of that upheaval, I was expecting our second child. I was sick the whole time and two of the nine months were spent right in bed. I remember how our Thai language informant sat beside my bed and tried to teach me. It was extremely hot and, as there was no electricity, there were no fans. A small generator provided lights only from 6 p.m. to 10 p.m., but the noise of the motor made my head ache and the smell of the gasoline from the generator increased my nausea. It seemed like a no-win situation.

I shall never forget two letters that our chairman, Rev. Robert Chrisman, wrote to me in those "terrible tone" days:

> *Dear Corrine,*
> *As a language student, you have my*

*special interest and sympathy. I have
noted that the language has been unusually difficult for you and that you have
that dogged determination to acquire it
that will eventually lead to success. I am
glad you completed your first year exam-
ination in a satisfactory manner and
that you have covered the most difficult
part of language study. In your case, as it
was in mine, Churchill's old ard famous
adage is true: "It is by blood, sweat, toil
and tears plus a lot of prayer that the victory is won."*

I'm not sure if his quotation from Churchill
was accurate, but it certainly was appropriate for
my situation.

His other letter arrived after I had failed my
18-month exam (one month after the Johnsons
were killed):

Dear Corrine,

*My heart goes out to you in a very
special way. I want you to know that I
have a deep sympathy for you and a deep
interest in you and in your acquiring the
language. When you have had an opportunity to profit by that more than a
month of language study you lost, let us
take the 18-month exam over again.
Don't let yourself get discouraged.
Maintain that dogged perseverance. There*

is no question in my mind but that you
will sharpen this invaluable tool for use
in winning souls to the Lord.

Nobody ever appreciated a certificate more than I did when I finally successfully completed the two years of language study. The certificate said, "This is to certify that Mrs. Corrine Sahlberg completed on January 27, 1953 all the requirements of the two-year Thai language course as prescribed by the Language School of the Siam Mission of The Christian and Missionary Alliance." It was such a relief to have language study behind me! It felt like a big bag of cement had been lifted off my back. Within days I went to Bangkok to deliver our second child.

Soon after returning to our station, I began speaking in children's meetings. The children didn't seem to mind when I made mistakes. Gradually my speaking improved to the point that I was able to teach adults when Elmer and the Thai pastor were away.

One Sunday after I had spoken, an old Vietnamese man came up to me. "You opened a door in my heart," he said.

I could have hugged him! I was communicating in the Thai language!

Some time later the same man asked my husband, "When are you going away again?"

"Why do you ask?" Elmer wanted to know.

"We like the way your wife teaches better

than the way you teach!"

I never could speak Thai as well as Elmer, but that day I learned that God could use even me in my own simple, basic language and teaching style. What a turnabout from the days of the terrible tones! Now, more than 35 years later, I sometimes even dream in Thai, a language I thought I would never be able to learn.

4

Shots out of the Darkness

My dear Mother,

It is with great sorrow that I write to you this morning [April 21, 1952]. You may have heard of the terrible tragedy that has happened here in Udorn, just 35 miles from our mission station. Priscilla Johnson was killed by several bandits as she was praying in a meeting out in a little village. Paul, her husband, was seriously wounded and had to be taken to the hospital. After the shooting, the bandits went into the house where the Johnsons' slept at night. They kicked little Billy (age 2) and stole many items. Becky (age 5) was also there. They tried to steal the Johnsons' Land Rover, but they couldn't get it started. Instead, out on the main highway, they stopped a truck, killed the driver and escaped in his vehicle.

Elmer and I went to the hospital to see Paul before he was flown to Bangkok.

He knew Priscilla was in heaven. She was only 31 years old—a wonderful worker for God. We had such good times together. I loved her like a sister and will miss her so much. We can't understand why something like this should happen.

Their oldest child, Bryan (age 7) is at the mission school in Dalat. The Johnsons were going to go home for their first furlough in just two months. Pray for us, Mom, and please don't worry. We are in God's will and we still have work to do here in Siam. Don't cry, Mom,—pray! Tell folks to pray. We need prayer.

That letter was followed shortly by another:

Dearest Mom:

"Beloved Paul with Jesus. Bringing body to Khon Kaen." That's the telegram sent from Bangkok by our Mission chairman to all mission stations. We are shocked because we expected Paul to recover from his wounds. Now he has been buried beside Priscilla. They have gone to be with the Lord instead of going on furlough. Three little children are left behind.

A week after the shootings, Elmer and I drove on the highway where the truck driver was killed by the fleeing bandits. We had to go on that road to get to the train station because we had been asked to go to Bangkok to help take care of Paul in the hospital. I'll admit I was afraid. The road was so dark. No houses around for miles. The bandits have not been caught. We sang hymns as we drove along. But we never did get to Bangkok. When the train made a short stop at Korat, Bill Carlsen met us there to tell us about Paul's death. We got off the train and returned to Khon Kaen.

Now, Mom, I have some news for you that might fill your heart with fear. But Mom, ask God to help you not to be afraid. We have been asked to take the Johnsons' place in Udorn until a missionary couple returns from furlough in about six months. The chairman feels that it is important to have missionaries live there to show we are not afraid. Right now, the Thai police are protecting the house. We do not feel we will need them once we live there.

Please don't worry about us, Mom. Pray for us and those who sorrow here in Siam and in the States. Little Becky and Billy have been told their parents are in heaven. Bryan is coming home from the school. All of them will travel to their grandparents with missionaries going on furlough.

Mom, we may not be in any danger at

*all, but if God should call us, we are
ready to go. We have work here to do.
Don't worry. God is able for every need.
Don't cry. We'll be praying for you, too.*

The Johnsons' deaths were a terrible blow to
us. We had shared many happy times with Paul
and Priscilla. They had become our closest
friends. As new missionaries, we looked up to
them as examples of what missionaries should
be. The Thai people loved them. Paul and
Priscilla fit right in with Thai customs and culture. They both spoke Thai fluently. They sang
together beautifully in both English and Thai.
Paul was very enthusiastic about preparing radio
tapes that were heard all over Thailand.

Right there, in the very house we were asked
to occupy, we had shared the Christmas holidays with the Johnsons. We did not know it
then, but it would be their last Christmas on
earth. On December 23rd, Priscilla entertained
about 20 Thai officials at a four o'clock tea. She
prepared many kinds of cookies and candy for
them. Paul invited the guests to see Christian
movies in the little chapel right across the lane.

Christmas Eve day was the special time for
missionary family celebrations. We feasted on a
traditional American dinner—turkey with all
the trimmings. Later, we opened gifts in the living room. Paul read the Christmas story and we
sang Christmas carols around the little artificial
Christmas tree.

Christmas Day was reserved for Thai Christians to join in a day-long celebration. About 35 of the 75 invited guests arrived the night before. They all slept in the chapel. Meals were eaten together on the huge porch of the Johnson home. Everyone sat on the floor according to Thai custom. The day's program had been well-prepared with morning meetings, a baptismal service, games in the afternoon and Christian movies at night. It was a wonderful few days of celebration.

When we first arrived in Thailand, the Johnsons had helped us get settled in our new home way up on the border of Laos. They were our nearest missionary neighbors. On our monthly shopping and banking trips to Udorn City, we always stopped at their house. We had great times together—eating, shopping and exchanging news.

Elmer and I were the last missionaries to see the Johnsons before the fateful night. They had made the two-hour drive to our home in Nongkai to make some tape recordings to send to the States. (There was no daytime electricity in Udorn.) After the tapes were finished, we chatted and decided to get together for an Easter dinner. They left about 8:30 p.m. I called out to Priscilla, "Be careful on the way home!" Those were the last words I ever spoke to her.

The day of the tragedy, Elmer left early for a short country trip. He planned to return at noon. This was most unusual as he often was gone days or even weeks. About mid-morning, a Thai postman came to our house. He said, "There is a phone call for you at the post office."

None of the missionaries had phones in their homes so I wondered who it could be. Maybe Priscilla was calling to change our Easter plans.

I hurried to the post office and picked up the phone. I heard a Thai man say something about "Mem is in heaven." I was still learning Thai and managed to piece together that Priscilla was dead and Paul badly injured. But I didn't know how it had happened. I didn't know the word for gun. Maybe there had been a car accident.

In tears, I left the post office. I got into a three-wheeled bicycle taxi and went a few blocks to the home of a Christian lawyer who spoke English. He went to the post office to find out what happened. It was then we learned that there had been a shooting in the village. At the lawyer's home, we all got down on our knees and wept and prayed for Paul and for their children.

I went home to wait for Elmer. As he drove past our house to take the evangelist home, I jumped on my bicycle to follow him. Elmer saw me following the Land Rover and stopped to see what was the matter. Tearfully, I told him the shocking news. We left immediately to see Paul in the hospital in Udorn.

On the way I said to Elmer, "I wonder if

Paul will remember the verse he wrote in his last letter to us: "The Lord giveth and the Lord taketh away. Blessed be the name of the Lord." It had been much easier to apply that verse in that instance (losing a bicycle) than in the present situation.

We walked into the little hospital room. Paul gripped Elmer's hand and said, "The Lord giveth and the Lord taketh away. Blessed be the name of the Lord."

Paul showed us the bandages covering the bullet wounds, then said, "I haven't cried as much as the rest of you. The Lord has given me a wonderful peace—a wonderful sustaining grace. We were praying in the meeting when all of a sudden there were gun shots out of the darkness. Priscilla jumped up, shouted and ran out to a clump of banana trees. Almost in the same instant, I felt something in my leg. It spun me around. Then I fell. There seemed to be eight or nine bandits. I saw three of them clearly.

"They took my watch and camera and then demanded a gun, which I didn't have. They wanted a gold chain, which I didn't have. I was bleeding profusely, so when they demanded the money in my wallet, I couldn't and wouldn't turn over because of the intense pain.

"Then they went to the house where we were staying and ransacked all our belongings. The children had been sleeping there. Becky came crying to me. The bandits tried to start the

Land Rover but the emergency brake was on and they didn't know how to make the car go. They killed the motor three times and then gave up. They fled, taking the keys with them.

"I directed some Thai Christians to look in my shaving kit for an extra car key. The bandits had shaken the kit but had overlooked the key. No one knew how to drive. I told them to put Priscilla in the car. They said, 'No need, Adjohn (teacher), better to leave her here.' I realized then that she was gone.

"The children and I got in the car and the people pushed it to a small village close by. There we met a man who knew a little about driving—enough to get us to the hospital. The servant girl stayed with me all night, fanning me and turning me over. The children stayed with the servant's family."

Paul continued.

"Take the lock off the garage door, Elmer, and put it on the book room. The bandits have the keys and if they go to the house, I'd like them to find some tracts and maybe they'll accept Christ." He also asked us to turn off the kerosene refrigerator and pay the Thai workers their wages.

Instructions completed, Paul's words began to drift away. His eyes fluttered. Quietly, we left the little room. We never saw Paul alive again!

Rev. Chrisman arranged for Paul to be flown to a hospital in Bangkok. Paul had requested that Mr. Chrisman remain with him. The children, with their Thai nursemaid, were flown to Korat to stay with the Bill Carlsen family.

Elmer and I left the hospital to do as Paul had requested. We put away some of the things they had taken on that last village trip. We disposed of the bloody mat that had been under Paul in the Land Rover. We discarded the shirt and trousers with the bullet holes. The little folding organ that Priscilla had been playing just before the shots rang out was sitting in the corner. The house was so quiet and empty. We just couldn't believe that Priscilla was dead and Paul so critically wounded.

At Paul's request, Theo Ziemer went to the village to get Priscilla's body. George Heckendorf, Clem Dreger, some Thai officials and a few Thai Christian workers accompanied them. Elmer and I drove the two hours to Khon Kaen to join the other missionaries gathered there, waiting for the body to arrive.

Near midnight, a truck with a police escort drove in with Priscilla's body. The governor of Udorn also arrived with his escort. Priscilla's body was placed in a coffin which had been made by the missionaries. Some of them took a last look at Priscilla. I did not. I wanted to remember her as I had last seen her—smiling and happy. The funeral was planned for the next morning at eight.

I'll never forget that service. We were all in a state of shock. I cried and cried as did many others at the graveside ceremony. Elmer had a part in the service. I had a part too, along with Johnnie Ziemer and Minnie Persons. We placed many bouquets of flowers on the grave.

Back in Nongkai, we were hoping for good news about Paul. But the news was not good. Paul passed away on April 23. The funeral service on Thursday, April 24, was held in the Khon Kaen Bible School chapel. Once again, we gathered at the Gospel Church cemetery for a commital service. This time, it was to place Paul beside his beloved Priscilla.

Each mission station had been sent a series of telegrams from our chairman. They tell the whole story of the shots out of the darkness:

"Priscilla shot and killed at Ban Donmafai while holding meetings. Paul shot and in Udorn hospital with broken leg. Bob, Theo rushing to help. Bob Chrisman."

"Paul underwent major operation. Condition serious. Pray, letter follows. Bob Chrisman."

"Paul very critical. Pray earnestly. Bob Chrisman."

"Paul underwent major operation. Condition serious. Come soon as possible. Khon Kaen to proceed Bangkok. Corrine help nurse and Elmer to drive Rover to and from hospital. Theo Ziemer." (This telegram was sent only to us.)

"Beloved Paul with Jesus. Bringing body to Khon Kaen. Bob."

"Funeral at Khon Kaen about noon Thursday. Bob."

The *Bangkok Post* of April 21, 1952, carried a

detailed account of the shooting under a head-line: "Two Missionaries Shot by Bandits." Both English and Thai newspapers printed in full Paul's words as he lay on a stretcher to be flown to Bangkok:

"May God forgive those who have killed my wife and wounded me. May He lead them to a place of repentance. As for myself, I am ready to die. I have served God to the best of my strength and my ability." Elmer and I made the move to the Johnsons' home in Udorn. Elmer, Ed Truax and I were appointed to dispose of the Johnsons' personal and household belongings. While I was sorting through their books, I found Paul's Bible school yearbook. The verse for his graduation year was First Chronicles 28:20: "He will not fail thee, nor forsake thee, until thou hast finished all the work for the service of the house of the Lord" (KJV).

Paul and Priscilla Johnson experienced the ultimate graduation in 1952. They had finished all their work for the service of the house of the Lord.

5

Widow with a Husband

Dear Mom,

We are all fine ["all" included our four children—David, Evelyn, Dale and Esther]. Elmer came home after being away 14 days. There was lots of work to catch up on—a door had fallen off the closet, an electric plug wouldn't work and we were out of most staples—rice, flour, sugar and other cooking supplies.

Again, in April of 1963, I wrote to my mother:

Elmer will be home a total of eight days this entire month. I do a lot of reading. I wouldn't mind having a TV!

Again to Mom in 1964:

Elmer has been gone three weeks. Won't be home for three more weeks!

Little Esther is good company. She keeps asking for Daddy. The children are okay—busy and happy at Dalat. It gets lonesome without Elmer here, but I keep busy making Thai teaching books, writing lectures and visiting our neighbors.

Married women missionaries of The Christian and Missionary Alliance are expected to be fulltime missionaries. That policy brought me face to face with two important issues:

1. What was my responsibility to the children God had given us?
2. What was my responsibility to the work God had called me to?

I settled those questions shortly after we arrived in Thailand, when our first son, David, was just a baby. I chose to work in the city where we lived. In the city I could give the best care to our children and also do my best work for God. I knew I was doing what God wanted me to do.

Making that choice, however, meant I would be alone with the children for long periods of time. Elmer's evangelism work took him far out into the country areas. That kind of life—rough roads, danger of robbers and poor living conditions—I felt, was just too difficult for the children. Finding suitable sleeping places and proper food for as many as six people, instead of one, would only complicate Elmer's ministry opportunities. Elmer could sleep almost anywhere and food was never a problem for him. So the "city missionary" and the "village missionary" learned to adapt. It was decided that when the last child went off to the mission boarding school, then I would travel with Elmer.

Coping with the "single-but-not-single" life was anything but easy. Just three months before the tragic death of the Johnsons, I took my first long train trip in Thailand without Elmer. I was traveling with two-year-old David while Elmer drove the Land Rover to our new home up on the border of Laos. The train left early in the morning and was scheduled to arrive in Udorn City at six that evening. Paul and Priscilla Johnson planned to meet me at the station. I would go to their home and Elmer would be there the next day.

Suddenly, however, the train stopped. I looked out the window. There was no station. All I could see were mountains and thick woods. Tall palms were silhouetted menacingly against the moonlit sky. *Why in the world would we be stopping in the middle of nowhere*, I wondered.

Soon a Thai conductor came through the car and stopped at our small compartment. David and I were the only foreigners on the train. The conductor said in English, "Train stop long time. You lock door. Close window.

Keep light out. Stay here."

I pulled down the shutters on the windows and locked the door to our little room. Peeking through the shutters, I began to understand why the conductor had warned me about locking the door. Some of the male passengers were outside pulling bottles of liquor from their pockets. The conductor, evidently concerned about a young white woman traveling alone, wanted me out of sight of those men.

As the hours passed, more and more people left the train to sit outside. A train wheel needed major repair. It was going to be a very long wait.

I became a little nervous. I could hear a party in process in the moonlight. I prayed that the drunken men would stay outside. David and I ate our leftover lunch sandwiches and drank from our water thermos. I was glad I had heeded the advice of an older missionary: "Always take water with you on trains, buses and in your own vehicle."

Around midnight the whistle blew and we were on our way again. The train pulled into Udorn at two a.m. Paul and Priscilla were waiting for me. They had made many trips to the station (there were no phones in those days). The station master could only say, "Train will be late!" At midnight, they decided to remain at the station so they wouldn't miss me. Elmer arrived the next day and together we headed for our new home in Nongkai.

There was certainly plenty of city work to do in Nongkai. I started holding children's meetings and when Elmer and the Thai preacher were away on village trips, I taught at the Sunday services and at the prayer meetings. It took hours and hours to prepare those lessons.

Another ministry began to develop for me. Students, nurses and even city officials requested English lessons. I told them, "I will teach you English, but I will use the Bible as the textbook." They agreed. Classes were held in our home and in government schools, still using the Bible as my textbook. I also spent hours selling Christian books and Bibles at our street chapel. The children and I talked to people, visited the food sellers along the sides of the roads and handed out tracts. Along the banks of the Mekong River, we watched the boats and chatted with the people who came to bathe there.

Looking forward to the time when Elmer and I would travel together in the villages, I prepared flannelgraph stories in large art books. But in spite of these ministries I was often frustrated. A November 1954 letter to our field chairman, Mr. Chrisman, reveals some of my deepest feelings:

> *I received a telegram last night from Elmer. First news in 17 days. The telegram stated, "Finished survey and meetings in Nongkai province. Now working*

*in Loei province. Feeling fine. Love,
Elmer."*

*Both of the children have had about the
worst colds they have ever had, but we are
all fine now. The Lord undertook in
answer to prayer. I continue to teach at
the services while a Thai girl watches the
children at home. Greet Mrs. Chrisman
for me. Tell her that when I start to feel a
little lonesome (no white faces here in
weeks), I think of how I planned to go to
the mission field as a single missionary.
Now, at least, I have Elmer some of the
time. I also have two children to keep
me company.*

Mr. Chrisman replied,

*Thank you for your letter. I am very
proud of you and others who often have to
do the hardest part of missionary work—
sticking by the stuff while others go.*

My journals reveal how I coped with "sticking
by the stuff" for weeks at a time:

November 1952: "Elmer plans a three-week
boat trip soon with two missionary men. That
will leave me the only American in this entire
area. I'm not afraid to stay alone, though I'll
miss Elmer. This is part of missionary life. Little
David is good company—chats all the time."

August 1953: "Elmer was off on a river trip

when I became ill with terrible sharp pains in my side. He came home earlier than he had planned. I believe God sent him home to help me and take care of the children. We can hear bombing going on across the river on the Laos side. Many people have told us it is dangerous to be in Thailand, but I'd rather die out here in His will [than be any place else]."

When the papers were full of news about a possible invasion of Thailand, I became concerned because we lived near the border.

January 1954: "I can still hear the bombs. Nongkai now has a special curfew. No one is allowed out after midnight or before five a.m. except with permission. No meetings of more than five people except with permission. Things are getting tense. Papers are full of the threat of an invasion. All kinds of measures are being taken to ward off such an occurrence. I am seriously considering moving down to Udorn but am waiting and praying to be sure this is God's will. If this area were to fall, I'd be the first missionary to know about an invasion! Soldiers would be at my door—no chance of escape. All the meetings have dropped in attendance; the chapel building might be sold. I might as well go to a place of safety. I think of the children. If I wait too long, it might be too late. I really hate to leave. Living at someone else's house will be inconvenient with the children, but maybe better than staying here. I wish I knew what to do."

I never did leave Nongkai.

February 1954: "I can still hear the bombing in the distance but I sleep soundly at night. It is no fun staying alone so much, but God does give me a wonderful peace. My place is with the children. Sometimes I feel I accomplish so little, but just being faithful is an important thing."

April 1954: "Elmer came home on Monday. He had planned to stay longer than nine days. I almost fell into his arms when he came in the door. I was at the end of my endurance.

"Evelyn has a terrible case of measles. As a result of walking the floor with her, my left arm pains so much I can hardly hold her. The well caved in. I had to have water brought in on carts. The chapel building was sold. The Thai worker who lived upstairs in the chapel has no place to live."

It was too much for me. I went to bed and Elmer took over. The baby got worse, but Elmer was there to walk the floor with her.

November 1954: "No lights and no Elmer! He has been gone almost a month. I am using kerosene lamps or candles until the city generator gets fixed. I am getting restless—a month is a long time to stay alone, but home is the best place for the children. Little Evelyn has been kissing Elmer's picture. The Lord is my peace and strength. I'm happy that Elmer is reaching those villages with the gospel."

Later that same month: "The lights were off three weeks. During this month I only saw foreigners three and half hours the entire month!"

Many, many times, over many years, I stood on the Mekong River bank and watched Elmer leave on a passenger/cargo river boat. I never knew if he'd be gone a week or a month. When he returned, we would hear all about the trip: "I spent two and a half days on a 12 by 12 foot bamboo raft. A trip through rapids on a raft is quite an experience! I don't know how the Thai men can judge the water so accurately, but they seem to know exactly when to start rowing to escape the huge boulders. I wished I could be as calm about it all as the cargo of pigs that accompanied us."

For a brief time, the Mission owned a boat, but from the beginning it was deemed to be "not correctly built for the Mekong River." Boats for Mekong River travel had flat bottoms. Ours was rounded. It was also "too high" and rocked precipitously when the current hit it. Eventually the boat was sold and Elmer was back to traveling on those creaky river boats. They were slow and maintained uncertain schedules, but at least they were safer than the Mission boat.

As furlough time drew near, I knew I needed a year in America. Four and a half years of life in Thailand had taken its toll. My journal records the frustration: "Another week and Elmer didn't come home. I am beginning to feel I can hardly stand another day alone. I'm discouraged with the poor attendance at the meetings. Although I keep busy, I am restless. I go for a walk every day. I feel I must walk. A lonely mission station is at times almost unbearable—so little to read, little (if any) mail (people seem to stop writing toward the end of a missionary's term) and no English programs on local radio stations. There is no one to talk with in my own language. Truly the Lord is a close Companion. If it weren't for the strength of the Lord and the everlasting arms, I could not stand the strain. The news reports are bad—trouble in Indo-China and talk of war with China. The heat is terrific. Lately I always feel tired. I do need a furlough. I'm more nervous than I used to be."

A week later I wrote in the journal: "I spent a lonely Easter. After the Easter lesson, I spent two hours at the boat dock waiting for Elmer to come. The boat did not arrive. Elmer came home the next day—by bus. The boat for Nongkai was not able to leave, so he had to find another way to get home. I was so happy to see him. I just cried and cried. He did not realize how lonely I was. He says he'll take shorter trips now. There is much work to be done in the villages close by. It is so good to have someone to talk to."

There were times when I was concerned about Elmer's safety. The fighting across the river alarmed me enough that I wrote to our chairman, Mr. Chrisman. He had always told us, "Don't take unnecessary risks." And so I wrote:

> *I told Elmer I would be writing to you about what I feel is an "unnecessary" risk. A United States Army man advised us to stay around home now as anything could happen. He told us that if an emergency arose we would probably get on a U.S. Army plane in Udorn. I am not afraid to stay alone—I don't feel nervous—but I am wondering about Elmer going off on extended river trips during this time. I feel it would be safer for him to work here in the city or in villages close by. Please let me know what you think.*

Mr. Chrisman answered,

> *It has been my intention to suggest that Elmer cease going on prolonged river trips. He should avoid overexposure to danger. While conditions are so uncertain, it seems wise to work in areas closer to home. I appreciate your eagerness to distribute the Word of God.*

On January 1954, Elmer wrote the chairman:

> *River travel is closed now because of what seemed to be machine gun fire on*

the river. I shall go only on day-long trips by Land Rover.

Later that year when the danger dissipated, Elmer was off again on river trips. On November 1954, obviously frustrated, I wrote my report to Mr. Chrisman:

Elmer has been gone about a month. His monthly reports and financial statements will be late. I refuse to do the station books because then he might stay out two months! Maybe, like Blondie in the Dagwood comics, I should have his suitcase ready with clean clothes as he dashes in and out of our house. Or maybe, since our Mission policy now is that single girls should not live alone, our conference ought to appoint another woman to live here!

I actually signed that letter "Miss" instead of "Mrs." because I lived alone so much of the time!

Although I was not usually bothered by fear, one incident remains fresh in my memory.

Elmer was out in the villages when trouble arose among the Vietnamese refugees in Nongkai. The government ordered the refugees to be fingerprinted, but they did not understand the reasoning behind the edict. Some of the men refused and were put in jail. So about

500 of their women gathered in front of the police station, squatting in typical fashion, to protest.

That night I could hear them screaming and crying all through the night (our home was only two blocks away from the police station). The next day, Saturday, the police used water hoses on the women in an effort to disburse them. I was the only American in the city and I knew that the Vietnamese did not like Americans. I sent a note with our Thai helper to the governor of the province. I told him that I was alone and asked him what I should do if things got worse. He advised me to stay inside the house and promised to send an escort to evacuate me if necessary. His assurance, as well as God's promise of protection, brought a measure of peace to my heart.

The loudspeakers were blaring an announcement: "All people who do not go home will be arrested." Then the message was directed to the local citizenry: "Thai citizens must stay off the streets. Be careful about drinking water from wells. There may be poison in the wells."

The next day, Sunday, I looked out of my window just as a group of wailing women were marched past our house. Six armed Thai policemen were forcing them to go back to their homes.

The government gradually got things back to normal and peace returned to the area. I was thankful for the people who prayed for us.

There were different ways of coping with the problems the children and I faced. I was happy for my medical training which helped when the children were sick. Also, I kept busy, not allowing myself to sit around and think about things I could not change.

Reaching out to other people kept me from feeling sorry for myself and I had the habit of walking every day. This discipline was good both for the body and mind. Photography, writing and reading helped me to relax. Besides all that, I never really felt alone. God was very real to me during those years.

I remember how surprised a woman in the States was when I responded to her question concerning how I faced problems on the mission field.

"Who did you go to when you had a real problem?" she asked.

I answered, "I went to God!"

"No, no," she replied. "I mean a person."

I explained, "Where I lived there was no one but God. For years, even my husband wasn't around much of the time. God was a very real Person to me. He met my needs."

As I checked through the 35 years worth of letters I had written to my mother, I was surprised at the length and frequency of Elmer's village trips. No wonder the Thai people called me *Maamy tee me saame*—the widow with a husband!

6

Golden Temples and Yellow Robes

One of our major concerns in Thailand was the challenge of rearing our four children in a non-Christian culture. As I explained in the preface, Buddhism was and is much more than the religion of Thailand. Its attitudes and axioms permeate every facet of society.

Christianity, of course, was and is much more than a religion. It is a way of life which centers on a relationship with the Lord Jesus Christ. It was that relationship that we preached and taught and lived before our children and others.

Shortly after our arrival in Thailand, the people celebrated the most important holiday in the Buddhist calendar—Visakha Puja—the Buddhist May festival. This event takes place each year at the May full moon. It commemorates the birth, enlightenment and death of Buddha. The temples are crowded and the streets filled with spectacular parades and beautiful fireworks.

Festivals and celebrations are an essential

part of Thai life. Almost all are in some way connected with Buddhism and are held at temples or on temple compounds. There are more than 26,000 temples in Thailand.

Bangkok, described by some as one of the most fascinating places in the world, is a city of magnificent temples with glistening golden spires and brilliant, sweeping roofs. Tourists by the thousands flock to see the Temple of the Emerald Buddha, the Marble Temple, the Temple of the Reclining Buddha and many other unique structures in the city.

Even in small villages beautiful golden temples can be found. Our own town of Nongkai had 28 temples. Thai people believe that merit can be accumulated by building or repairing temples. Their entire way of life revolves around Buddhism. Ninety-five percent of Thai people are Buddhists. Buddhist concepts mold their speech and pervade their thought patterns. Buddhist codes determine morals and conduct.

Buddhists do not believe in a personal God but believe that each person must trust in himself and earn his own salvation. They believe that merit-making balances their misdeeds and ensures a better life in the next reincarnation. Nirvana is their highest goal—no more rebirths, only eternal bliss.

In addition to the care and building of temples, merit can be gained by attending temple services on holy days, placing a thin gold leaf on an image of Buddha, giving gifts to priests or performing religious ceremonies. The most common way to make merit is to offer food to the priests.

Every morning, yellow-robed priests walk single file down the streets, stopping at homes and shops where people with deepest respect give them gifts of rice, curry and sometimes sweets. These are placed in the large bowl which each priest carries.

Another significant way to make merit is to become a priest. The Thai believe that every man over the age of 20 should enter the priesthood. In this way, merit is not only accrued for the man himself, but also for his parents. He may remain a priest for only a few days, a few months, many years or even a lifetime. Boys who enter at the age of 10 are called novices. They may, at age 20, go through an ordination ceremony to become a monk. An article in a Thai magazine (May 1979) stated that there are at any one time over 200,000 monks and novice monks in Thailand.

Almost all Thai celebrations, civic or personal, require the presence of the monks. They chant passages from the Buddhist scriptures and give their blessings as they sprinkle holy water on people or objects. They are present at the opening of new homes, new schools, new stores, new buildings and all kinds of community projects. Thai people offer food and gifts to the monks before wedding ceremonies, on birthdays and at all special occasions. If there is a death in the family, the monks chant as the deceased is cremated on the temple compound.

Huge statues of Buddha dot the country-side—in the sides of mountains, on top of mountains or along the edges of the road. The great abundance of these images and their position of respect in temples, schools, stores and private homes attest to their importance in Thai culture.

Spirit houses are in the corners of almost every yard, on roof tops, in stores and hotel compounds. Usually up on poles, these miniature temples, the Thai believe, become the dwelling place for the spirits that inhabit that plot of land. To keep the spirits contented, the people bring daily offerings of food, flowers and incense.

Many Thai have great faith in the power of amulets and charms to protect them from harm or to provide good fortune and well-being. Often worn on a neck chain, these charms are usually tiny Buddhas which have been blessed by a priest.

Although Buddhism is the official religion of Thailand, the government allows the people to profess any religion. Section 25 of the Constitution of the Kingdom of Thailand grants this religious liberty and protection. Thai kings must be Buddhist, but they also possess the title of "Protector of All Religions." In 1976, a 50-page booklet, published by the Department of Religion of Thailand and explaining Christian doctrines, was distributed to the people.

Although we lived in and our children grew up in this culture, we never participated in any Buddhist ceremonies. We taught the children to respect the Buddhist religion, but of course we wanted them to follow the Christian way—to believe in Jesus Christ as their personal Savior. In our home, at boarding school and in the Thai churches they were taught to read God's Word, to pray and to live the Christian life.

We did enjoy the delightful festivals, however, especially the one called Songkra which is held on April 13, the Thai New Year's Day. This is known as the Water Throwing Festival. After offering food at the temples in the morning, the people make their annual pilgrimage to their ancestors' family pagodas. They clean and sprinkle scented water on these memorials. Then they go to visit relatives to pour scented water on the palms of the elders and give them gifts. In return, they ask for and receive a blessing. After all this, the water throwing starts. Anyone who dares to venture outside will no doubt get wet. The water throwing signifies a hope for rain for the coming rice planting season. In country areas, the festival may go on for several days.

Another celebration which our family enjoyed was the Loi Krathong Festival—the Festival of Lights. This festival is celebrated on a full moon night in November. The Thai go to temples and light candles and lanterns around the compound. Then they float little lotus-shaped boats made of banana leaves down the rivers, canals, lakes and ponds. Each little boat contains a flower, a coin, some incense sticks and a lit candle. It is a beautiful picture to see the hundreds of lights twinkling in the darkness. The festival always concludes with a dazzling fireworks display.

According to a Thai writer, one of the purposes of this festival is to entreat Mother Nature to carry away the sins of the people in the little boats. It is also significant as a means of thanking Mother Water for her bountiful gift of rain.

In the midst of this strong Buddhist influence, Elmer and I told the story of Jesus. We often heard people say *muan gun*—"the same"—the story of Buddha and the story of Jesus were the same. When we read from the Bible about the miraculous birth of Jesus, they would say *muan gun*, for, according to tradition, Buddha also had a miraculous birth.

When we talked about the wisdom that Jesus had as a child, we were told that Buddha was also a child with great wisdom.

Our account of the temptation of Jesus made no impression on them, for Buddha was also tempted.

Even our stories of the miracles that Jesus performed were similar to the records of the miracles of Buddha.

Jesus commissioned men to go preach. So did Buddha.

Buddha knew when he would die, even as Jesus knew the time of His death.

It seemed that we were making very little impact with our message until one day, when we explained the resurrection of Jesus. No one dared to say *muan gun*, for Buddha did not rise from the dead. He is not alive. Only Jesus Christ lives.

A particular teacher in a small town often told us, "It's the same." One day, we went to visit him. We made a special point of explaining the resurrection of Jesus and left literature for him to study.

When we went back the next day, he said, *My muan gun.*—It's not the same!

He was right. It's not the same. Christ is alive! It is that message that we went to Thailand to deliver.

7

Little MKs

In 1959 I wrote:

Civilization has finally come to Nongkai. Now we can ignore the old well in our yard because the city just installed a water system. Our drinking water now comes out of faucets, but the water must still be boiled or filtered. The children are having a time adjusting to flush toilets. They are used to dipping water from a large clay jar. Even the shower is new to them. Most of the time we dipped cold water from a storage container. We did have a pulley system rigged up for hot water, but the water first had to be heated in a kettle. A large metal container had to be lowered, filled and pulled up. A lever released the hot water.

Nongkai is changing in other ways too. We even have a railroad line coming right into the city. Buses, that used to run only when they were full, now go out every hour on the hour.

During the early years in Thailand another thing we lacked was overseas telephone service. Telegrams were the only means to inform our relatives back home of any important news. My mother received three very special telegrams from Bangkok, Thailand:

In 1953:

> *Evelyn Joyce arrived at 1:30 a.m. on February 25 by emergency Caesarean section. Baby and Corrine doing fine.*

In 1957:

> *Dale Bryan born April 25 by Caesarean section. Mother and son doing well.*

In 1960:

> *Esther Sylvia arrived November 15 by Caesarean section. All is fine.*

Letters always followed the telegrams explaining the details of the births. I realize now how very difficult it must have been for my mother to wait for those telegrams. She knew that the only reliable medical care was in Bangkok, hundreds of miles away from where we lived. Train service did not extend to Nongkai, so each "baby trip" began with a two-and-a-half hour ride over very rough and bumpy dirt roads. It was a miracle that the babies were not born somewhere on that road! Then it was a 13-hour train ride from Udorn to Bangkok. In May of 1957 I wrote to my mother:

> *I thought I would surely die before I got to Bangkok! When I arrived, the doctor would not schedule the Caesarean section until my type of blood was available. Elmer spent a lot of time ᴖhecking around for a suitable donor. Fiᴖally, John and Ruth Perkins donated blood. Our Mission nurse, Honor Warden, was assigned to stay with me during the operation and for several days after.*

Bringing up children in the primitive conditions of the years before "civilization" came presented its own set of challenges. For one thing, there were two languages—Thai and English. We always spoke English to the children. We felt that they needed to learn English thought patterns as well as English vocabulary. But there were no other white children in Nongkai, so their playmates were all Thai. Our yard became the neighborhood playground and it wasn't long until our little MKs were as fluent in Thai as in English. To this day, all four of our children speak Thai without an accent.

In the early years, toys, and especially dolls, were scarce. I remember making a cloth doll for Evelyn and stuffing it with rice. Even now,

when I pass all the beautiful dolls in department stores, I think of the times I longed for
one of those dolls for my girls. It was impossible
for friends and family to send toys because of
the heavy import duty.

Every child needs a three-wheeler. Each of
our children had one—but it was the same
one—just painted a different color for each
child. In 1965 I wrote to my mother:

> *I just repainted the little three-wheel
> tricycle that we brought out on the ship
> [15 years earlier] for David. We also
> replaced the wheel. The children play on
> the cement patio under our living quar-
> ters, away from the hot sun and rain.*

We usually had dogs, both as pets and as
watchdogs. One especially memorable one was
a Doberman pinscher named Sheba who was
given to us by a former U.S. Army man. We
had no problems with robbers for the 10 years
that Sheba lived with us.

Our farmyard collection increased. "Dear
Mom," I wrote,

> *Out in our back yard are two beautiful
> horses—a mother and a colt. We got both
> for only $15. We also have two dogs, three
> cats and four chickens (we get fresh eggs
> now). There is a large fishing pond way
> in the back of this property. The chil-*

dren caught some good-sized fish back there.

Another letter in 1966 informed Mother of certain other additions to our menagerie:

We now have a tame deer for a pet. A Navy man and his wife leaving for the States gave it to us. This deer, called a barking deer, stays about the size of a large dog. Bambi (the deer) roams our fenced-in front yard. We built a shelter for it to go into at night. We also have two parrots. I am teaching them to talk.

Monkeys, too, were added to the list—ordinary ones as well as a beautiful gibbon that the children called Paddie.

Although we were surrounded by another culture, we always celebrated the American holidays. One Thanksgiving, I made place cards of paper pumpkins for the table and bought little Chinese counting boards so the children could count their blessings.

A manger scene was always the focal point in our home at Christmas so the children, as well as visitors, would realize the true meaning of Christmas. The manger was made from an old wooden box turned upside down. Drilled holes held the pegged flannelgraph figures which we pasted on heavy cardboard. We also constructed a small Christmas tree from bamboo poles, wire and green crepe paper. Decorations made from Christmas cards made our little tree quite attractive. All these symbols gave us the opportunity to explain the true meaning of Christmas in a land where there is no Christmas.

We often hosted a Christmas party for the Thai Christians, complete with games and refreshments. Some years as many as 300 students came to our home in groups on Christmas Day. Each one received a tract, a Christmas story booklet and some candy.

To keep our English/American culture alive for the children, we made sure that our shelves contained books which included American classics, fairy tales, missionary stories, animal and adventure stories. We read to our children each night, beginning with a missionary biography followed by a devotional or Bible story book. Our daughters still have some of those books in their own homes. In addition, we always subscribed to *TIME* magazine and *Reader's Digest* to help us keep informed of life on the other side of the world.

Our family truly enjoyed living in Thailand. Although we adapted as much as we could to the local way of life, we wanted to be sure the children would be able to fit in with American culture when we were on furloughs and later when the time came for them to go to college.

A testimonial to how well we accomplished that goal came when David's first grade teacher in America said to us: "We gave your son an entrance exam with many questions. He did so well on the test that I can hardly believe that this boy has not lived in the United States!"

During another furlough we received a call from Esther's first grade teacher.

"I want to tell you," she said, "that you need to check on your daughter's vivid imagination. In our geography class we discuss different countries. Esther always says, 'I've been there.' She claims to have traveled all around the world. I am concerned about this and want to let you know what she had been telling us."

Elmer asked the teacher the names of the countries that Esther claimed to have visited. When the teacher told him, he said, "She has been to every one!"

8

Goodbyes at Bangkok Airport

Dearest Mom,
    The children left yesterday for Malaysia to return to school. I was so tired—still am. So much excitement. Forty-four children. Eighty pieces of luggage. Quite a scene at the airport. None of our three children cried, though Esther and Dale almost did. The children seemed glad to be going back to a school routine, their friends and parties! I will return home to Korat on the train. Elmer will not be there as he is traveling with Rev. King. The house will really be empty.

Elmer and I knew when we accepted our appointment to Thailand that the policy of The Christian and Missionary Alliance requires wives to be fulltime missionaries and that children of missionaries attend boarding schools. This policy was determined after careful research and much prayer. Of five possible options, the Mission boarding school was considered to be the best for the children and for the parents.

The options were: (1) Home-schooling via correspondence courses through to the last year of school; (2) Home-schooling to the eighth grade, then the children would go to hostels in the U.S. or Canada for high school; (3) Local schools with teaching in the native language; (4) Secular international schools located in large cities throughout the world; (5) Alliance boarding schools providing education from first to 12th grade.

Each option had its own weaknesses: (1) Most missionary mothers are not qualified teachers. Children need not only book knowledge, but a well-rounded social life and the competition and challenge that come from being in a classroom. (2) Children would be away from parents for long periods of time; adequate hostels are difficult to find (and very expensive); short terms of work disrupt missionary programs. (3) Speech patterns of another language would be learned. Most local schools teach by rote and do not teach children to think for themselves. (4) Many missionaries live far from international schools. Hostels would have to be set up. The cost of such facilities plus tuition would be prohibitive.

After these and other considerations were

taken into account, it was concluded that our Mission boarding schools provide loving care given by carefully screened personnel who are called by God to serve in those capacities. Our schools conform to the highest standards of North American education. Missionary children often are capable of doing exceptionally well in advanced entrance exams. In the case of my family, framed graduate and post-graduate degrees and certificates hanging on our office wall testify to the excellence of the education they received. David holds a Master of Arts Degree in Education; Evelyn, a Degree of Juris Doctor (she is a judge in Ohio); Dale, a Bachelors Degree in Business (computer analyst); and Esther, a Bachelor of Arts and Certified Surgeon's Assistant degree.

As Elmer and I traveled in the villages, the Thai often asked me, "Where are your children?"

I answered, "They are studying at our Mission boarding school."

Their response was, "How nice! So easy for you."

They were so wrong! It was never easy to send our children away to school. In fact, that is the most difficult part of missionary life.

Through the years, one by one, the children went off to school. Goodbyes over those years were never easy. Many parents wore sun glasses at the airport to hide their tears.

In a letter dated June 1956, I wrote to my

mother:

> *David [age seven] flew alone to the school in Vietnam as the other children had already gone. He told us he wanted to go alone. We had just traveled halfway around the world, he said, so this short journey was something he could handle without us! We made arrangements for some missionaries to meet him at both stopovers—Pnom Penh and Saigon. When the plane arrived at the Dalat City airport, a staff member was there to meet him. I wish you could have seen him at the Bangkok airport. He was so proud to be going alone. He even forgot to kiss us goodbye before he marched up the ramp. Then he remembered, so he came back down! Never shed a tear! He didn't even look sad! We put him the in care of the steward on the plane.*

We were relieved when a telegram arrived telling us that David had arrived safely in Vietnam. We never would have sent him off alone if he hadn't wanted it that way.

Going to school by plane was a way of life for our children. The schools were located hundreds of miles from where we lived. Only during one brief period that the school was in Malaysia could train transportation be used. When the railroads became targets for

Communist attack, all the children went by plane.

On January 12, 1959, I again wrote Mother:

> *We thought Evelyn [age six] would be happy to go to Dalat as she seemed to be looking forward to it. But at the airport she cried and clung to me. She went to the plane holding tightly to her big brother's hand. Her tears flowed. Once she is at school she will be okay. This is for the best. We must adjust, but it isn't easy. Those first six years are so special to us because we know the time of parting comes. So we return to our work in Nongkai.*

A few weeks later, the school nurse, Lois Chandler, wrote to say that "Evelyn was getting along fine."

Another letter to mother dated July 7, 1963:

> *Now three of our children have flown off to school. Dale [age six] seems to doing fine away from home. He seemed to enjoy going—didn't even cry. But I did! It was difficult to send him off, but the Lord gave me peace. I'm glad he has a sister and brother there with him. Little Esther will be lost without him.*

Later that month, July 26th:

Dale enjoys school. The dorm mother told us that he is always asking questions and he is so interesting. Big brother David keeps an eye on him. He wrote us that Dale obeys very well at school.

Esther, our youngest, began school in the U.S. while we were on furlough. Then, on our way back to Thailand, we stopped by the school and the last child was left there.

I wrote to my mother in July 1968:

We are safely back in Bangkok. Even though we landed and took off so many times, it was a wonderful trip. We left the children on Monday at the school in Tanah Rata. We helped Esther unpack and get settled in. Then we had to say goodbye. Esther started to cry. Evelyn put her arm around her to comfort her. Dale waved to us. And now we are back to the work.

Later, Evelyn wrote us that after we were gone she took Esther and Dale to the store for a soda.

Most children accept boarding school. Others have difficulty coping with roommates, rules and a life regulated by bells. Dale wrote:

The get-up bell rings at 6:30. At seven, another bell for breakfast. Then we go clean our rooms and at the sound of the

*eight o'clock bell we go to class. At noon,
another bell for lunch. Then a bell at
1:10 for afternoon class. We get out of
classes at 3:15. Then we go swimming,
play tennis, basketball or just have fun.
At six o'clock, another bell—for supper.
One more bell—lights out! Dorm life is
okay. I have four roommates.*

While writing this book I found an essay
written by one of our children for a ninth grade
English class.

*When you go to a boarding school, life
isn't easy at times. You don't really have
anyone you can talk to—like your parents. When you have problems you have
to try to work them out by yourself. At
home, you can be more free to be yourself.
Your parents accept you for who you are
and what you are. You begin to miss
your parents a whole lot but you even forget what they really look like and what
they are like. Many different kinds of
problems arise because of close living in a
boarding school.*

The children attended boarding school nine
months out of each year with two vacation
periods in between—one in the summer months
and one during the Christmas and New Year
holiday time. The stateside curriculum used at

Dalat required a certain number of days in school. As long as those requirements were met, the opening and closing dates of school could be adjusted.

Vacation times were always extra special for us all. I explained this to my mother:

> *Our family is once again complete. We try to spend extra time with them. They are home so little and growing up so fast. We took a four-day trip back up to Nongkai where we lived for eight years. The children have so many friends there. We visited in many Thai homes and left tracts and books with each family.*

And again:

> *We are having a wonderful vacation together here at the seashore. I think that we enjoy our times more than most American families because we are separated so much. We go fishing, rent paddle boats, play miniature golf and swim by the hour. Elmer is far away from all office duties. We will return home on the 20th of December. I already prepared everything for Christmas. The tree is up, gifts wrapped and all the cards are mailed. I won't be rushed when we get back home. We are having a lot of fun here.*

In January 1964 I reported another family

trip to mother:

The Land Rover was crammed full—a family of six needs a lot of things for five days out in isolated country villages. We took along our umbrella tent. Six can sleep in it—four in a row with the two little ones at our feet. Crowded, but we managed just fine. We took canned goods and large plastic containers of water, plus suitcases, teaching materials, flashlights, sleeping bags, pillows, a first aid kit, a few pans, dishes, eating utensils, a pressure lamp and a small pressure stove.

We left at 9:30 a.m. to travel the 90 miles to the home of a Thai evangelist for our first visit. We ate our noon meal at a small Chinese shop—rice, fish and fried meat with vegetables. The villagers stared at the funny foreigners. At supper time, we all sat on the floor in the home of the evangelist to eat supper with him and his wife and eight children.

The next morning, we went on to a small village. We had to take an ox-cart trail through rice fields and up over some dikes. At the village, we were told we could set up the tent in an unfinished house—no walls but the floor was up off the ground. We had to climb a ladder to get to the tent. Crowds gathered to watch us put it up. Some boys even climbed into the surrounding trees to get a better view. We used our canned food as no other food was available there.

Some of the Thai young people taught the kids to walk on stilts. At night, we held a service in their little wooden chapel. We slept comfortably in the tent high above the ground.

On we went to another village—over an even worse trail. I held my breath as we crawled slowly up and down deep ridges. Again, crowds of people stared at us. This time we put the tent up on the back porch of a Thai home which was up on poles.

We had to ration our water because there wasn't even a well in this village. We used dirty pond water to take a bath. We had Sunday services there. All the inconveniences were worth it. Three young men accepted Christ as their Savior.

The next village was only eight miles away. We set up our tent under a shady tree and hoped it wouldn't rain too much. People watched our every move. Fifty to seventy-five children (and adults too) squatted in front of our tent. Evelyn [then age 11] said, "This is like being on television!" Dale [age six] resented the crowds and shouted, "Make them stop looking at me!" David [age 14] always helped with setting up and taking down the tent.

> *Esther [age three] was a great attraction because of her long blonde hair.*

Our airport goodbyes spanned the years from 1956 to 1978. With four children, each almost four years apart, it meant that the last one started school when the oldest was in college. Finally, in 1978, we went to the Bangkok airport to send Esther back to Dalat for her last semester.

I wrote my mother:

> *We sent Esther off on a plane to Malaysia—the last time for her to go to Dalat. It is also the last time for us to send a child to school. I'm glad that part of our lives is finished. Twenty-two years of airport goodbyes are enough.*

We had gone to the airport four times a year for 22 years! We never did get used to it!

During the years in Thailand we had two other farewells at the Bangkok airport, not for children leaving for Dalat but for children leaving us to go to college in the United States. These farewells, which encompassed not months but years—four years to be exact, were extremely difficult. But God gave us peace as we commited each one to Him.

In 1979, Elmer and I returned to Thailand after our furlough. We had never gone to Thailand without at least one child. Three of the children were at the airport in Tampa, Florida, to say goodbye. I am sure the people in the boarding area didn't expect the older couple—us—to get on the plane. In Florida, older people are usually the ones who say goodbye as the young ones fly back north. This time the tables were turned. It was now the children seeing us—their parents—off to Thailand for our final term.

9

The School That Kept Moving

Dearest Mom,

What a week! I just returned from Bangkok last night. On Sunday morning we sent our two boys off on the plane to return to school. With all the fighting going on in Vietnam we found it difficult to let them go. However, the American Embassy informed us that it was all right to send them. Can you imagine how we felt as we heard a radio broadcast announcing that President Johnson was ordering all American government dependents to leave Vietnam and that Communist forces had attacked American bases?

How we wished we had never allowed the boys to go! I don't know where they are—in a plane returning to Thailand or at school in Vietnam. These are days of

*tension and strain for all of us. We just
want them out of Vietnam. We can figure
out later what to do about their education. I'm so glad Evelyn isn't there too.
She is still in Bangkok with the Cases
getting her teeth straightened.*

*Elmer, as chairman of the field, has
great responsibility concerning all the
Thailand children. Pray for us. We live
one day at a time.*

Nine days later, I wrote again:

Dear Mom,

*Elmer flew to Saigon for conferences
with Rev. King, Grady Mangham, chairman of the Vietnam field, Gene Evans,
director of Dalat School and some U.S.
Embassy men. They discussed the dangerous situation at the school because of
the new threats. The decision was made to
keep the school open for a while, but
plans were made to evacuate the children
and staff if things get worse.*

*Elmer brought Dale back home when
he returned. There is a lower grade
American school here that he can attend
for a while. A few other Thailand children
also returned with him. Their parents
had requested their return. I hope all the
children leave soon. I wish David could be
here. I know you are concerned, too. These*

are anxious days for us.

In view of the worsening situation in Vietnam, Elmer went to the Department of Education and the Department of Foreign Affairs in Bangkok to make plans to set up a school. He obtained permission from the International School to integrate with their school. Some property in Bangkok belonging to the American Club was leased on April 15th. Elmer Wehr, principal of Dalat School, and his wife Ruth, met with authorities of the International School to discuss arrangements.

The American government had four C-123s in Vietnam ready to evacuate the children and staff to Bangkok. Buses and trucks were on hand to transport everyone to the airport. We listened to the news and prayed. Even though the Viet Cong had been fighting for years, this was the first time the school had been threatened.

Already in 1963 I had been concerned about having the children in Vietnam. I wrote my mother then:

> *We have really been on edge these last few days with all the fighting and uncertainties of the war. As far as we know, the children are okay. Their vacation time will soon be here. Maybe things will get better before they return to school.*
>
> *Only a few weeks ago, President Diem*

*visited the school. He was shown David's
room as an example of how the children
live at the school. Evelyn took pictures of
him with the camera you gave her. Now,
according to the latest news reports, he is
dead! This part of the world is full of
uncertainty. We must keep a firm faith in
God.*

Two years later, on April 30, 1965, I sent
this good news to my mother:

*Dear Mom,
David is in Bangkok—thank God!
First a telegram came on Sunday afternoon: "Children flying to Bangkok in
four plane loads on Monday the 19th."
We also heard the news on our short wave
radio: "One hundred and eighteen children and teachers have been evacuated
from Dalat, Vietnam. They are the sons
and daughters of The Christian and
Missionary Alliance workers in Southeast
Asia." The front page of the Bangkok
English newspaper headlined, "Evacuated
from South Vietnam," with a picture of
some of the students and a teacher at
the airport.*

Later we learned why the school was evacuated. A pre-dawn attack close to the school
had caused the deaths of eight American ser-

vicemen and the wounding of over 100. American planes had then bombed strategic staging areas.

That evening, Gene Evans called for a meeting in the school auditorium and briefed the group about the attack on the American base. Then he announced that he had received a letter from Rev. Sahlberg, chairman of the Thailand field, requesting that all children of Thailand missionaries be sent back to Thailand. The Thai field MKs were ordered to be packed and ready to leave the next morning.

In the morning, a radio announcer reported the deaths of 21 more American soldiers at an American military base. This time, the whole school was ordered to pack and be ready for evacuation on short notice. On Monday night, the students heard what they thought was the sound of mortars and howitzers. Were the Viet Cong soldiers attacking the school? They eventually learned that it was just target practice by a military academy. But the students and staff were justifiably nervous.

Conditions within Vietnam continued to deteriorate. Elmer flew to the school to attend the annual board meeting. The board discussed the threat to the school and finally reached a decision—the school would be evacuated.

At four o'clock on Sunday afternoon, all students and staff were summoned to the auditorium once again. Grady Mangham made the announcement: "After much prayer and careful consideration, the school board and Rev. L.L. King, president of The Christian and Missionary Alliance, have decided that Dalat School will be moved to Thailand."

So began the saga of "the school that kept moving."

The first move, to Bangkok, was a happy one for all the Thai missionaries. We would see our children more often.

Some months after the move, I wrote to my mother:

> *Maybe you saw on television how the airport at Dalat was shot up last week. I'm so glad the children are out of there.*

And again, November 23, 1965:

> *We just learned that the school is moving again—this time to Malaysia. There is little hope of returning to Vietnam. Bangkok is too expensive, too hot and too crowded. Play area is very limited. During heavy rains, the classrooms and even some of the bedrooms flood. Serious visa problems have resulted because Dalat students come from many different countries.*

A spacious resort hotel with a large playground area was rented in the beautiful mountains of the Cameron Highlands in Malaysia where the year-round temperature averages 65 degrees. It seemed to be an ideal location. School opened in January 1966 at Tanah Rata. The students liked the cooler weather and especially enjoyed hiking in the surrounding jungle areas.

But in 1971, the Dalat School (as it was and is still called) moved again—this time to the oceanside resort of Sandycroft on the island of Penang in Malaysia. Sandycroft had formerly been a British military rest and recreation center. The move was made because the Tanah Rata location proved to be too isolated from doctors, hospitals, dentists, cultural activities and recreational facilities. Also, the mountain road to Tanah Rata boasted over 500 curves!

Ah, those curves! Many a student had gotten sick going around those curves. Esther wrote us in 1970:

> *We had a nice trip up to the school. We didn't see any accidents. Near the end of the trip I threw up. Two bags! The bus ahead of us had trouble. All the kids had to get in our bus except some older boys who walked the last two miles.*

Sandycroft, four times the size of the mountain campus, provided the space needed for classrooms, dormitories and play areas. All other facilities were just six miles from the school in Georgetown. The school is still enjoying that beautiful location, today.

Children at the school are required to write to their parents every Sunday afternoon. This good habit starts at age six with the help of the dorm parents. How we waited for that weekly letter! However, we never knew what we would find. The news could be amusing, puzzling, sad, happy, informative or alarming. The alarming letters usually had a note enclosed from a dorm parent, teacher, nurse or doctor. I was always nervous about opening the thick ones. Lois Chandler, the school nurse, faithfully reported all medical problems. She took care of all four of our children from the time they started school in Vietnam until they graduated.

MKs become independent and self-reliant at a very early age. The letters from our children were good indicators of how they coped with and adjusted to life in boarding school. Peek over my shoulder at excerpts from letters we received from nine-year-old Esther, 12-year-old Dale, and 17-year-old Evelyn.

From Esther:

> *I used my real heavy blue sweater for sleeping. On Saturday, Lolly and me went on a hike and we saw two monkeys, one in a tree. But we scared them away. I like school and the food.*

From Evelyn:

> *I have top bunk. Six blankets, some*

doubled. I sure miss you both. We painted our bed yesterday. It was all rusty. We put two trunks on top of each other and made a dressing table. We used a white sheet, a pink pillowcase, and put white lace on top of that and it looks so pretty. We came home from a mountain hike in the dark. We had a few flashlights. Dale wasn't very generous with the one he had. I yelled at him a few times and he yelled at me and I fell on the bridge. I also got two bloodsuckers on me. Uck! It was loads of fun.

From Dale:

I miss you but I am glad to see my friends. We went on a hike—48 kids with six or seven flashlights. Almost lost. We cooked wieners and had other stuff with it. Well, keep me informed of home real well.

From Esther:

Friday night we went up to Tomson's Plato (Thompson's Plateau). We ate supper and then we played games. The boys slept in two big tents. Some of us hiked home in the dark with Miss Chandler and Miss Craddock. The rest of the kids went in the van. It was real fun. I used my new boots five times. I skate a lot.

From Dale:

How is home? I'm doing fine up here. Been getting good grades and stuff. On Friday we went on a hayride. Two trucks came and took us to a lake near a power dam. There we sat around, sang songs and stuff. Games and a real fine windy ride home. It's been cold up here. Lots of rain. Real cool and cold. Fine. Different from Thailand. Got a fine room and roommates. Staying out of trouble. Sure do miss you guys.

From Evelyn:

Hi. I had a real nice birthday and party. I had it after supper in Miss Chandler's apartment. Blazing fireplace. I had white cake and frosting with real flowers over it. I invited the junior girls and the Khon Kaen kids. Many gifts. Were mainly things to eat. I feel older too. Miss you loads.

From Dale:

I'm in photo club and I'm working hard on my stamps. I've got to hurry because I am past time getting this letter in. I suppose you guys are really going all over Thailand. I'm going in the jungle. Except I don't "save" the tigers! I'm learning the guitar. Be seeing you in your letters.

From Evelyn:

> *Some good news for you, Mom. This is snake season. They have found loads of little ones all over and this week some boys saw a ten-foot one and caught a six-foot one. It was monstrous. They chopped its head off. It was probably of the boa constrictor family. They have made a rule now that no one under sixth grade can go for a hike or into the jungles without an adult along until the snake season is over. You might include this in your prayer letters. Esther seems to be getting along okay and hasn't gotten into any trouble that I know of. I cut Dale's hair for him now; saves money and he is happier cause they don't scalp him any more.*

From Dale:

> *Staying there, all alone*
> *Don't you wish we were home?*
> *Come up here, the weather's fine*
> *Makes me want to write this rhyme.*
> *Work's much better, play the best*
> *And all the rest is filled with rest.*

While our children learned to cope with their

feelings, we had to cope with ours, especially when we received a letter such as this one written by 11-year-old Esther:

> *This semester is too long. I have been very homesick. I cry each night. Here is a song my roommate and I made up:*
>
> *Come and sit by my side, my dear parents*
> *Do not miss my bright eyes and bright*
>   *smile*
> *Just remember the school that I go to*
> *And the daughter who loves you so true.*

We were relieved when the next letter came:

> *I prayed to God to comfort me so that I wouldn't get homesick. Now I don't get very homesick.*

Graduation time and the weeks preceding it were always extra special at the school. The senior assembly, a recital, track meet, choir concert, senior party, staff tea party for seniors, parents' banquet, talent night, baccalaureate, senior breakfast, exams and projects all had to be fit into the last 17 days before graduation. All four of our children graduated from Dalat School and Elmer and I were there for each ceremony. Elmer, as chairman of the school board, had the honor of presenting David with his diploma.

Were there any problems associated with the school? Yes, of course. In one instance especially, when I felt that the circumstances were just too much for me to cope with, God gave me a message from His Word (Psalm 40:2-3): "He brought me up also out of an horrible pit, out of the miry clay, and set my feet upon a rock, and established my goings. And he hath put a new song in my mouth, even praise unto our God: many shall see it, and fear, and shall trust in the Lord" (KJV).

In this most difficult time, God helped us in very special ways. He did set my feet on the rock and He did guide me in the right direction. In time, a new song did come to my heart.

As missionary parents we owe much to the dedicated teachers, dorm parents, directors, nurses and staff at Dalat School who cared for and taught our four children. They were the facilitators who allowed us to carry on 35 years of missionary work in Thailand.

10

I Am Going to Kill You

Dearest Mom,

It is hot today—too hot to move! Esther is playing with her Thai friends. She can really rattle off the language. Elmer went out into the jungles. It is getting danger-ous in the country areas. In addition to the ever-present robbers, bands of com-munists now rove in places where we once traveled as a family. I will not go in those areas. I get too nervous.

The choice had been made—I was the "city missionary" and Elmer was the "country missionary." Elmer felt a tremendous bur-den for the village people. Entire villages had never heard of God's plan of salvation. We were the only missionaries in a province of 144,000 people, so the weight of the responsi-bility rested heavily upon us.

The Mission sponsored the Gospel of John House-to-House Campaign. The goal was to place a Gospel in all the homes within our area of responsibility. The booklets contained a lesson sheet with an address where interested people could mail the lesson and receive other lessons. The team which traveled with Elmer helped distribute these free books and also sold other Christian books and Bibles at low cost.

The following letters to our chairman are revealing. In 1952, I wrote:

> *The children and I watched as the team headed down the river. In a few days, the bookseller came back for more Bible tracts and brought a letter from Elmer telling how the people beg the team to stay in their village to preach. Elmer gets permission for a meeting to be held in the central meeting place. The team is welcomed wherever they go. These villagers have never heard about Jesus.*

Later, Elmer reported:

> *I made an 18-day boat trip stopping at numerous villages along the river. Thousands heard the gospel for the first time. We left over 25,000 pieces of literature with the people. Everywhere large crowds gathered to hear the message.*

Another progress report to the chairman:

> *On a 13-day trip we gave out Gospels*
> *of John in 22 villages, 16 of which were*
> *new places where we had never gone*
> *before. Some villagers were afraid of me as*
> *they had never seen a white man before.*
> *Some wondered why we were giving out*
> *free books. But many came to the night*
> *meetings to hear us explain the gospel*
> *story. This year, a total of 149 villages*
> *were covered house to house. Almost*
> *17,000 Gospels of John were given out in*
> *those places. Many of the villages heard*
> *about Jesus for the first time.*

Nongkai province, over 160 miles long and 20 miles wide, had only 14 miles of road and much of that road was covered with water during the rainy season. So traveling to the villages was difficult and included travel by foot, oxcart, bicycle, raft, assorted boats, the Land Rover (and later a Toyota pickup), bus, pony cart and even by elephant.

An elephant was used only once. In Loei province, Elmer and Wayne Persons hired an elephant for a trip into the mountains. It was a slow ride and every time they reached a stream, the elephant would fill its trunk with water and shoot it over its back to cool itself. It also cooled Elmer and Wayne! That was the last and only time they traveled by elephant.

A 1953 trip was unforgettable. Elmer wrote,

Wayne Persons, Ed Truax, some Thai Christian men and I traveled in two Land Rovers to visit the Hmong tribespeople in the mountains of northeast Thailand. It took three full days to go 52 miles over very rough mountain roads. We camped in a tent near a little stream and ate boiled chicken and sticky rice. The first night out, the Thai pastor was awakened by the sound of a tiger roaring close by. He quickly got up and lit a fire to scare the animal away.

We left the vehicles at a village at the base of the mountains and hired a guide to take us to the village. We walked two full days through dense forests and cold streams. It rained heavily the whole time. Leeches attached themselves to our arms, legs and feet.

We finally arrived at the first village. They did not understand Thai but understood the Lao dialect which Wayne and I knew. They also understood Chinese which Ed Truax spoke. A meeting was held at the chief's home. After a night's rest, we went on to another village. Five more hours of hard walking—three of those hours straight up mountains! The evening service was well attended. We slept in the home of the witch doctor. All around us and over us were his ceremonial articles—bloody feathers on a stick, a

*small drum and other objects of pagan
worship.*

*In both villages, we noticed people had
crosses on their clothing. They could not
explain the origin of these crosses but
told us that they were worn as a sign of
trust in a goddess of mercy sent to them
by an angel many years ago. In the first
village, all the women wore trousers. In
the second, all the women wore white
skirts with black blouses. Women and
men in both villages wore silver rings
around their necks. Their wealth determined the number of rings. The tribal
houses are right on the ground and are all
without windows.*

It was on the way back from this trip that
Elmer had to wait for a swollen stream to go
down before he could get home. Meanwhile, I
was waiting too—in Bangkok—for another baby!
Another report:

*Elmer rode the bicycle 17 miles each
way through terrible roads to go to a
meeting. At times he even had to carry the
bicycle—too much mud or water. He will
go again soon for some special meetings.
Can't even get a Land Rover in there. No
wonder he doesn't gain weight!*

One night in a remote village along the

Mekong River, a crowd of 200 or more gathered to hear Elmer preach. As they sat on the large porch of the meeting place, Elmer showed them pictures from a picture roll. All of a sudden, seven men pushed into the crowd. One marched right up in front of Elmer and said, "I am going to take you out and kill you!"

Elmer responded, "Please sit down and let me finish preaching first." Strangely, the man sat down on the floor beside the head man of the village.

The head man turned to the stranger and said, "The governor has requested that I protect this missionary. Don't you do anything to him."

That enraged the robber. Angrily he replied, "We will take you out, too, and kill you with the missionary!"

The threat was too much for the bodyguards of the head man. Two of them pounced on the robber and the men of the village jumped on the other six. All seven were tied up. In an amazing way, God had intervened in what had been a life-threatening situation. Elmer told me later that he had no idea why he had asked the man to sit down and allow him to finish preaching. It just popped out of his mouth.

There were other experiences with robbers, too. A man in a certain village was most anxious to have Elmer and the team come and hold meetings. The Land Rover, however, could not make it over the terrible road, so the team turned back. On the way home, some people informed them that the man who invited them to the village was really a bandit chief who probably was planning to rob the team once they got to the village. Two Thai team members decided they would walk to the village, and thus arrive unnoticed. At the village they found out that the robbers were indeed looking for "the American" and planning to rob him. In this instance, God used impassable roads to protect His servants.

On another occasion, Elmer and a Thai pastor were out in a village along the border holding meetings. Elmer noticed three policemen watching the proceedings from a distance. When the meeting was finished, one of them approached him and asked to see a written permit for preaching. Elmer told the policeman that he did not have anything in writing, but that he did have verbal permission from the assistant governor. The policeman responded, "We must take you to the police station."

The policemen, each carrying a tommy gun, got into the Land Rover along with Elmer and escorted him into town. The officers at the border station decided to take Elmer to the chief of police. Elmer waited nervously outside while one of the policemen went in to explain the situation to the chief. In no time at all the policeman came back outside.

"Sorry. It is all a mistake," he said. "You have permission to go anywhere you want to go. I shall inform all border police."

The chief of police had recognized Elmer. "Teacher Sahlberg" now had the most official permission to preach and give out literature in all of Nongkai province!

11

Snake in the Grass (and in the Bedroom)

We weren't in Thailand very long before we had our first encounter with a cobra. In fact, we drove a Land Rover right over it. We thought it was just a small tree trunk lying across the road. Instead, the head of a very angry red-hooded cobra suddenly appeared over the driver's side of the half door. The tail—hold your breath—was flipped up on the other side of the vehicle! It was one tough snake. The jolt of the back tires plus the weight of six people should have stunned the snake. Instead, the 10-foot-long creature simply slithered away into the jungle!

Some years later I reported another snake incident to my mother:

> *Last Sunday afternoon Elmer thought he was imagining things. From behind the dresser in our bedroom appeared the head of what proved to be a huge snake. Elmer called to me, "Don't come in here!" He*

*jumped up on on the bed and after sur-
veying the situation, carefully crept out of
the room. He got a long-handled spade
and put on knee-high boots. Now armed
and ready, he couldn't find the snake!
However, as he poked at some clothes on
a hook, the snake sprang from behind
them and struck at the top of Elmer's
boots. He managed to kill the snake. It
was three feet long. The neighbors told us
the snake was poisonous, but not deadly.
It probably could have killed a child.*

*I cried and cried. In only a year and a
half we have killed over 25 snakes outside
and three (deadly ones) inside the house.
I told Elmer we would have to move. I am
about at the end of my emotional rope.
Every night I check the whole house before
we go to sleep. I always carry a flashlight
at night, even inside the house. We have
to have a young Thai girl watch Esther
every minute or else she must stay with
me. The ponds and canals around this
house must breed the snakes. Elmer
nailed up some of the loose wall boards
and put in more screening. We are also
starting to look for a house in other areas.
Today I found a baby snake in the bathroom. It was a viper—deadly. Pray for
us—for me. I need it!*

With Elmer's permission I wrote to the

Mission field committee:

> *I cannot stay in this house for another*
> *rainy season because of the snakes here.*
> *There have been over 25 snakes outside*
> *and now four inside. It is especially dif-*
> *ficult with a young child and I am under*
> *constant tension. Many of these snakes*
> *have been deadly. I expected to see snakes*
> *in Thailand, but not so many!*

Before we had a chance to find another house, Elmer was chosen to be the new chairman of the Mission. That meant a move to a different city. After we moved into the new house, I wrote my mother:

> *It surely is a relief for me to be here in*
> *this house. I can even let the children*
> *play outside.*

One of the worst snake experiences happened when I was at home with the children and Elmer was out in the villages.

The Thai helper came running in one day and said, "The dog is barking at a big snake in the back yard."

I went out to check. Right there, where I had walked just minutes earlier, was a long snake. The helper went across the street to get the neighbor.

The neighbor came. He took one look at the snake and said, "Get inside the house—everyone!" With a long iron bar he struck the snake seven or eight times. Finally, he was able to kill it. He told us to be very careful as there could be a mate close by.

I found out later that the snake was a rare spitting cobra. We had heard of spitting cobras. An American soldier at a nearby airbase had been temporarily blinded by the spit of such a snake. They can spit up to six or eight feet. We had also heard that the skin rots where the spit falls. We were so glad to have a dog who warned us many times about snakes in the yard.

In our field magazine, *The Task*, I quoted the following excerpt from the Bangkok English newspaper: "Statistics show that more people are bitten by poisonous snakes in Thailand than anywhere else. Between 300 and 400 Thais are killed by poisonous snakes every year. Most are victims of pit vipers, cobras, or banded kraits."

In my journal of 1953 I wrote,

> *I sometimes put Evelyn outside in her playpen, but seldom leave her alone. If I do, it is only for a few minutes. I always think of scorpions, snakes or other dangers. This past Thursday, I went to the kitchen for only a few minutes. When I came out, there on the steps not two feet from the baby was a little snake. I grabbed her from the playpen and retreat-*

*ed to a safe distance. I shouted for Elmer.
A Thai helper got there first and killed
the snake. He said it wasn't poisonous,
but it could have been. This is life in
the tropics. We must always watch and
commit ourselves to the Lord's care. We
also found a huge scorpion in the bathroom right where we shower.*

In two different letters, many years apart, I
told my mother, "I am so tired of snakes!" I
think I hate snakes even more than most people
because of a childhood experience. I was only
six years old when I saw my five-year-old brother bitten by a snake. The snake was not poisonous, but my fear of snakes started right
then.

Snakes were certainly a major problem in
Thailand, but life in the tropics had other difficulties too. We had to constantly fight termites as well. Thailand termites seem to be a
special breed, appearing quickly and doing
extreme damage behind the scenes.

In our first wooden house in Nongkai, we
noticed a small dirt trail going up the sides of
the large center posts of the dining room. Elmer
tapped on the posts. They sounded hollow.
Upon further investigation, we discovered that
the termites had destroyed almost the entire
dining room! All the walls, posts and even the
ceiling had to be replaced after a chemical
treatment of the house.

Once, returning home from a vacation, we heard a buzzing sound as we entered the house. Enough termites were eating away in a bookcase full of children's books that their presence was audible at the door! Many beautiful books had to be thrown out and I spent days repairing ones that could be salvaged.

In another house in Khon Kaen, I had placed about 20 books on a shelf over a staircase. We went up and down those steps regularly and never saw a sign of termites. One day, however, I pulled a book out. The whole inside was eaten out! In fact, almost all the books were totally destroyed—full of dust, crumbled pages and stacks of termites. Only the bindings remained intact.

The termites even bored through a steamer trunk in a screened-in porch. New sheets, blankets and towels that I had saved for the children to take to boarding school were filled with small holes, chunks of dirt and, of course, the termites.

In addition to snakes and termites, there were also small lizards and larger ones called dukgaas that ran up the insides of the walls of our houses. I didn't mind the little, harmless ones, but the larger ones that could give a nasty bite we chased out.

All this was part of life in the tropics. These experiences did not make me wish I had never gone to Thailand. But they did make me thankful for people who prayed for us and for God's watchful care over our family.

And, yes, I still hate snakes and I always will!

12

From the Farm Field to the Mission Field

Dearest Mom,

I have a wonderful surprise for you. Elmer has been chosen to be chairman of the Thailand Mission—the highest honor that a missionary can receive. It came as a surprise because there were other experienced missionaries. But Elmer was chosen. One of the things he will be responsible for is the safety of our Thailand missionaries—a heavy burden in itself because conditions in the area are not good. He will also be responsible for all Mission money and will represent the Thailand field on the Dalat school board. That means he will get to see the children often.

We will be moving to Korat and will have the same address we had when we first came to Thailand.

There will be some adjustments for me to make including doing a lot of enter-

taining (something I have never really enjoyed). I also know that people in positions of leadership are subject to criticism, so I'll have to learn to cope with that. But at least Elmer will not be off in the jungles!

As a young farmer in Minnesota, Elmer had expected to farm for the rest of his life. He and his brother, George, had operated a dairy farm until 1941 when Elmer was drafted into the United States Army.

"I was drafted into the army just before Pearl Harbor," Elmer wrote in a 1951 article. "The shock of the bombing there aroused a great fear in my heart—a fear of the future. I even bought a Bible and decided one night to attend a Bible study and prayer meeting at the army chapel. After the meeting, an army master sergeant, Tom Shakespeare, asked, 'Elmer, are you a Christian?'

"I answered, 'I'm trying to be one.' He knew then that I was not! He explained the plan of salvation to me using John 3:16 and that night I accepted Jesus Christ as my personal Savior.

"A few weeks later I was on my way to combat in the Pacific Islands, but now I had real peace in my heart. During my 31 months there, I had the opportunity of seeing missions in action. I did not know it then, but I later realized that God was speaking to me about becoming a missionary.

"During three months in the hospital with a neck and spinal infection, the chaplain told me about an organization called The Christian and Missionary Alliance and the work they were doing around the world. He suggested that I contact them and check into getting some training for missionary service. It was there in New Zealand that I finally decided that if God wanted me, I would be a missionary.

"When I told my family, they asked, 'Why do you want to be a missionary?' They were surprised to learn that I did not intend to go back to the farm, especially since plans had already been made to do so. I told them that I had personally witnessed the transformation in the lives of many of the island people. I could not forget the man who said, 'Won't you come back and help give out the story of Jesus?'"

Elmer finished his four years of service and rather than going to the nearby St. Paul Bible College, he entered Nyack Bible College in the spring of 1946. Our Mission rule at the time was that missionaries had to attend Nyack College for their final year. Elmer did not wish to begin at one school and transfer later to another, so he had chosen Nyack over St. Paul. I always said that God sent him to Nyack because I was there! I was a third year student preparing for foreign ministry. I never would have met Elmer if he had attended college in Minnesota.

By taking summer courses, Elmer was able to graduate just two years later. After graduation, he headed to Prattville, Alabama, at the request of Rev. T.G. Mangham, Sr., the district superintendent who had recommended Nyack College.

Elmer pastored there alone for six months until I completed a nursing course in New York City. We were married in Oceanside, Long Island, on November 13, 1948.

Mission policy required all missionary candidates to have two years' experience in a church at home before going overseas. We spent a happy two years together in Prattville and eventually the telegram with our appointment to Siam arrived.

In September 1950, Elmer, little David and I left the U.S. aboard the *S.S. Steel Navigator*, a cargo ship. Fifty-seven days later we arrived in Bangkok, Thailand, with its "cobras in the kitchen, bandits in the jungle and communists across the river."

13

Please Don't Let My Daddy Die

Dearest Mom,

I'll be so glad to get back to the U.S. Drivers are just crazy in this country. Every trip here is like going on a Coney Island cyclone ride! Rules mean nothing. Every man for himself! Speeding and racing. There are bicycles, motor scooters by the dozens, dogs and people in the streets. Some roads are full of holes. Even the U.S. Army men here are afraid to drive. They said they have never seen anything like it. You would have to see it to believe it!

Riding in a three-wheel taxi (samlaw) is even more dangerous. I have had four narrow escapes, so I refuse to use them anymore. The train is a lot safer.

I became unusually fearful on the roads because of what had happened the year before. On December 5, 1966, the highways of Thailand were extra crowded because it was a special holiday—the king's birthday. Our family had been invited to a retreat at a seashore resort in southern Thailand where Elmer would speak to some American servicemen. We drove from Korat City to Bangkok, a four-hour trip. There we joined the convoy going to the seashore—four hours more on the road.

Since the soldiers seemed to enjoy visiting with an American family, we decided to divide ourselves up between the three buses. Elmer and Dale got on the first bus and Evelyn (13), Esther (six) and I rode on the second bus. David (17) rode on the third bus. Usually I was terrified riding on buses in Thailand but an American soldier was driving, so I felt relaxed.

It was a beautiful sunny afternoon as we headed south toward the beach. As we rounded a very long curve on the narrow road, I saw an overturned bus up ahead with smoke rising from it. In one sickening moment, I realized that it was one our buses. I shouted, "My husband and son are on that bus!"

The driver braked and pulled up a short distance behind the overturned bus. Some of the men jumped out to help. Before I could get to the front of our bus, a soldier arrived with nine-year-old Dale in his arms.

"Stay here, ma'am," the soldier said. "Your husband is badly hurt. Take care of your son. He has some cuts."

I looked at Dale. He had some cuts on his leg

and one eye was injured. I took some bandages from my little first aid travel bag and put them on Dale's leg. I didn't know what to do about his eye. I noticed that some soldiers were blocking the doorway of the bus to prevent me from going to Elmer.

Suddenly, without warning, Dale jumped up, knelt on the front seat of the bus and put his head on the cushion.

"Dear God," he prayed loudly, "don't let my daddy die!"

An instant hush came over the bus.

Soon, some soldiers came to explain that a large, oncoming truck had crowded the first bus to the side of the road where it hit a pothole. A front spring broke and the driver lost control. The bus hit a bridge and turned over. Elmer, they said, had gone headfirst through the windshield and struck the cement bridge surface.

"Your husband is badly injured, but he is alive," they assured me.

As one of the men handed me Elmer's shoes, he told me that Dale had tried to grab on to his father as he saw him heading for the windshield, but that Elmer's shoes had come off in his hands. A soldier had in turn grabbed Dale to prevent him from going through the windshield too. David, who had been riding in the third bus, was taking charge of getting his father to the hospital as he was the only other adult on the buses that spoke Thai.

David flagged down a passing car and asked them to take Elmer to the nearest hospital. Thai people do not usually allow accident victims into their cars because they fear the spirits of anyone who might die en route. This driver, however, had served in the Korean War, so he agreed to take blood-splattered Elmer and our son to the hospital in a nearby town.

After the car left, the soldiers allowed me to go and look at the overturned bus. By this time, a crowd of curious onlookers—American soldiers and local Thai—had gathered, staring in silence. I walked to the bridge and surveyed the front of the bus. Broken glass was everywhere. The road was covered with blood. I knew it was Elmer's blood. I prayed that God would spare his life.

We got back on the bus and headed to a town about 30 minutes away. The chaplain assigned three soldiers—all close family friends—to stay with us and help in whatever way they could. The others went on to the retreat.

As I walked, dazed, into the hospital, a young American approached me.

"I am with the Peace Corps," he said. "I heard that some Americans were in an accident. I came to help."

"Where are we?" I asked.

"You are in Phetburi," he answered.

I remembered that the Buchers, missionaries from another Mission, lived in that town. I asked the young man if he could find them.

"Oh, I know them," he responded. "I'll go get them."

The soldiers stayed with the children and our luggage while I went to look for Elmer.

I found him in an examining room. A Thai doctor and some nurses were painstakingly removing glass shards from his head. As the doctor stitched together a large gash, he asked me some questions. Learning that I was a practical nurse, he asked me to wash the blood off my husband.

"The hospital is full," he explained. "We have no nurses available to care for your husband. You must assume that responsibility and watch carefully all night for any signs of brain injury. We do not even have a place to put him except in a chart room. We will try to find a room tomorrow." I assured him that I would help in any way possible.

The Buchers arrived within the hour. They took the four children, the three soldiers and all of our luggage home with them and provided food and a place to sleep for everyone. They brought food to me and later to Elmer (Thai country hospitals do not provide food service). They also helped me notify the Mission headquarters about the accident.

Elmer remained in a coma all night. The next day, after he regained consciousness, he was moved to the only available place—a room in the children's ward. A special duty Thai nurse came to take my place so I could take off my bloodsplattered clothes and get some sleep.

The following day, Elmer was taken by ambulance to a large hospital in Bangkok—a two-and-one-half hour trip over rough roads. Doctors were waiting there to check the head injury. The children (Dale's wounds were healing nicely) and I returned to Bangkok by train.

Before we left Phetburi, I offered the Buchers some money. Mrs. Bucher said, "Once we were in an accident in a strange place in the States during one of our furloughs. Some people helped us and when we went to pay them, they said, 'Pass the kindness along.' So we are doing that just now."

Within a year, we too were able to say those same words to an American couple who were involved in an accident near our home in Korat.

After a few days in intensive care in Bangkok, Elmer was moved to a private room and Mission nurses provided round-the-clock care. Elmer was experiencing considerable pain as a result of a some broken ribs. In addition, a concussion was causing severe headaches.

One day, a Thai preacher friend came to visit Elmer at the hospital. He prayed that Elmer would be free from the headaches. To the amazement of the doctors, the headaches left. Elmer has not had a headache since that time! Praise the Lord!

Did God answer the prayer of a little boy on the front seat of a bus? Yes, He did! About two weeks after the accident, the neurosurgeon told me, "It is an absolute miracle that your husband is alive!"

Elmer and Corrine Sahlberg, 1991.

Each furlough over the years we gave out prayer reminder cards. This was the one for 1962. From left to right: Corrine with Esther, Elmer with Dale, David behind Evelyn.

Together again in 1983 in Florida. From left to right front row: Evelyn, Elmer, Corrine, Esther. In back left to right: David and Dale.

We got back from furlough too late for David to go to our Mission school on the plane with the other children. He insisted on going the 1,000 miles alone.

Esther watching Thai food being prepared. All of our children enjoy Thai food more than American food.

Our children were part of our team. Little Dale does his part at our bookstall at a fair.

Scene from the early days in Nongkai. Little Evelyn standing by Elmer was a big attraction on one of our first long trips in Nongkai province. The people there had never seen a white child.

I always wanted to walk, not ride, across bridges like this one—and there were many.

Our first assignment was to work in Nongkai province along the Mekong River. We lived in this house nine years—the longest time in one house during all of our years in Thailand.

Sitting on those hard, backless benches for hours was difficult. But sharing the gospel was a great joy.

Tent set-up for a five-day campaign. It held 500 but usually 600–800 came. They crowded in at the sides and back of the tent.

During the years of tent campaigns we had a home away from home. Crowds always gathered when we cranked up our A-frame folding travel trailer.

A typical Thai greeting. We learned to follow their custom of leaving shoes at the bottom of the steps.

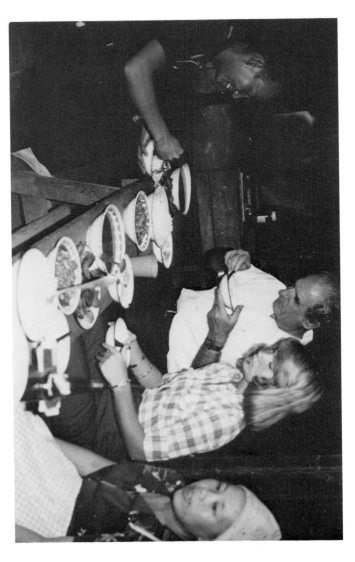

Elmer and Esther share a meal with Christian refugees from Laos in one of the several refugee camps.

Climbing rickety steps was a way of life for me during our village trips. I'm dressed in my "village missionary" outfit.

Wherever we traveled, I displayed Christian literature for sale at discount prices. Thai people like to read.

I always enjoyed talking with the village women—sharing blessings and problems.

Paul and Priscilla Johnson with Billy, Becky and Bryan, taken seven months before they were martyred. They had sent this picture to all the Thailand missionaries at Christmas time.

Elmer, with Betty Mitchell and her daughter, Geraldine, at the Bangkok airport after Betty's release from prison in Hanoi.

God gave me the privilege of being with my 86-year-old mother for her last Christmas on earth, 1982.

14

Dr. Jesus

Dear Grandma,

I'm writing this for Mom. Last Saturday she was taking down the curtains in my bedroom to wash them. She climbed up on the sewing machine to get the curtains off the rods. One rod sprang back and threw her onto the floor. Although she landed on her back, she managed to hold her head up so it did not hit the floor or the dresser. Her spine compressed like an accordion. We didn't move her until the doctor came.

We took her to the Thai hospital in our Land Rover. They took four X-rays at the hospital. She has two fractured vertebrae but she is not paralyzed. Her insides were badly shaken by the fall and stopped working for a few days. She is in a lot of pain and has to take pain pills. She is feeling better now.

The Thai doctor is the only orthopedist in Northeast Thailand. He arrived here in Khon Kaen only two months ago after

*five years of training in America. Dad
canceled all his meetings so he can be
with Mom. I stay with her at night
because they don't have enough nurses.
It's a good thing we kids were home on
vacation when this happened.*

*She sends her love and says not to
worry.*

Love, Evelyn

This unexpected turn of events provided yet
another opportunity for us to put into practice
something that had become a priority in our
lives—trusting God as our Healer, as the One
who could meet all our physical needs.

I was suffering considerably because of the
fractured vertebrae and the effects of the fall.
The doctor had told Elmer that I might even
need an operation to restore all the organs to
proper function.

In the meantime, however, a Thai Christian
woman, Mrs. Nong Noo, a close friend of
mine, came to visit me. She knelt by my bed
and prayed simply that God would heal me. She
had hardly left the room when I fell into a
deep sleep. To my surprise and relief, I wakened
some hours later completely free from pain,
with all organs operating. I knew that the fractured bones had instantly mended!

The Thai doctor was very surprised when I
told him that I had absolutely no pain. He
canceled the order for the steel back brace that

he had ordered shipped up from Bangkok. When I arrived home, our own Mission doctor examined me and he, too, was amazed at my recovery. He said, "God has performed a miracle in healing you."

Later, Elmer told me that he knew God had touched me when Mrs. Nong Noo prayed. God's presence had been in the hospital room in a most unusual way.

Divine healing was not an unusual experience in our family. It had become a natural thing for us to turn to God in times of sickness and distress.

I remember a time in Florida when I called Meals on Wheels to ask them to supply meals to my 85-year-old mother. The man on the other end of the line asked her, "Who is your doctor, Mrs. Henricksen?"

She replied, "Dr. Jesus."

The man asked her to spell it, no doubt thinking that the doctor was probably Spanish. I later explained that Mother always asked God to heal her and that she had never had a family doctor—only Dr. Jesus.

Dr. Jesus was our doctor in Thailand, too. In March 1952, I wrote in my journal:

David became very sick on Monday night. Because of the diarrhea, high fever and constant vomiting, we feared he had cholera. We had special prayer by his bed. When we finished praying, he vom-

ited again. Then he said, "I want to sing!" He sang the chorus of Step by Step *in Thai and immediately started to get well.*

I remember another time when David vomited bright red blood. This had never happened to anyone in our family so we were very alarmed. We tried to pray but I found it difficult because my heart was filled with fear of what could happen. In the midst of my turmoil, I remembered that friends in America had promised to pray for us. Some had told me that when they were unable to sleep they prayed. Sitting by David's bed, I felt prayer surround me like a cloak. The next day David was well. Dr. Jesus had made a house call at our home. I often wondered who was upholding the Sahlberg family in prayer that night.

Many times, with Elmer off on long trips, I had to cope alone with various crises. No phone, no missionaries close by, no family doctor. The small hospitals in our area did not meet even the most basic American sanitary standards. In Bangkok there were excellent hospitals, but they were two-days' journey away by train. I was thankful for the medical training I had received at Booth Memorial Hospital in New York City. God often gave me wisdom beyond my understanding and intervened in our circumstances:

One night David woke up wheezing and breathing with great difficulty. I thought he might die. I prayed and I cried. After about ten minutes, he began to breathe easier. He then dropped off to sleep.

Little Evelyn has such a bad cold that I am afraid she will choke. I prayed and God answered prayer. She slept well. Elmer has been gone a week now.

I'll never forget opening a letter from Dalat School and reading that Evelyn had broken her arm in a fall from a tree. My heart ached to be with her even though I knew she would receive the best of care. A Vietnamese doctor from the area set the bone. All we could do was write letters to her and pray for her.

Within weeks, another letter came from the school informing us that Evelyn had to be flown to Saigon to see a bone specialist. She was having a lot of pain in the arm. Dr. Ardel Vietti, the school doctor who had not been there during the accident, accompanied Evelyn on the plane. Dr. Vietti felt that the bone had been incorrectly set. The American specialist in Saigon decided not to reset the bone since there was some improvement. He advised us to check with a bone specialist in America when we went on furlough. We did that and he, too, agreed it was best not to operate. The arm had greatly improved.

Many years later we learned that a group of women in the States had prayed for "the little girl who broke her arm at Dalat School." Dr. Jesus had heard another prayer.

Telegrams from Dalat School almost always meant sickness or accident. In November 1970, one of those telegrams informed us that Esther needed an operation on her foot because two lumps were growing rapidly and were causing numbness. The school authorities wanted to know if the operation should be done there or did we want to wait until the Christmas vacation break to have it taken care of in Bangkok. We wired them to wait.

The Mission doctor, Dr. Garland Bare, checked the foot. He advised us to go to the Bangkok hospital since there was a possibility of cancer. Two American doctors operated the next day. The biopsy showed no signs of cancer—only fatty tissue. It took 11 stitches to close up the wound. She needed a cast up to her knee.

Another lump appeared seven years later, this time on the same leg by her knee cap. Back we went to the same hospital in Bangkok. After X-rays, the doctor operated on what he thought was a simple bone spur. But it wasn't a spur at all—it was a tumor. The biopsy again showed no sign of malignancy. Dr. Jesus had been present again.

I, too, was told I would have to have an operation when a doctor discovered a lump in my breast during a routine medical checkup. The possibility of cancer scared me and I was finding it very difficult to cope with that thought. Alone in my room at the Bangkok guest home, I opened the Bible, seeking a special message from the Lord. Psalm 56:13 (KJV) jumped off the page: "Wilt not thou deliver my feet from falling that I may walk before God in the light of the living?"

The phrase "of the living" seemed especially appropriate and encouraging. Peace came to my heart. The doctor operated that week and removed a cyst and two tumors. The lab test indicated no sign of cancer. A later pathology report confirmed "no malignancy present." The doctor told me that the tumors were the kind that could have caused cancer had they not been removed in time. We thanked God for showing His loving care once again. Even though we lived so far away from good medical facilities, He guided us in our times of need.

Elmer, too, found that Dr. Jesus was there when a scratch caused blood poisoning in his arm and when he broke his wrist in a fall. God helped us in coping with these and many more medical problems. He touched and healed us many times. Dr. Jesus was always there.

15

In the Middle of a Revolution

On April 1, 1981, I wrote to Evelyn [in America],

By the time you get this letter, I hope things settle down here, but right now we are in the middle of a revolution. Troops are on the move from here in Korat to go help fight in Bangkok. The royal family is here with the prime minister. Right now as I write, the leader of the revolution is in control of Bangkok. Daddy is down there too on Mission business.

I just heard that there are clashes between the opposing groups going on now on the road between here and Bangkok. I keep the radio on all the time. It is difficult to keep calm in these circumstances. I think that the prime minister here will regain control. Don't worry. I'll write to Grandma and tell her not to worry too.

As I reread the many letters written to my mother over the years, I suddenly realized how many times I had written, "Don't worry about us." Poor Mom—she never knew what to expect in those thin, blue airmail folders!

> *Dear Mom,*
> *We turned our radio on this morning only to find that there has just been a coup. I thought you might worry about us if you heard about it on your TV. But there is no need for that—everything is under control. No need to be concerned. We'll keep you posted on the news.*

On April 3rd, the radio station announced the victory of the government forces. The prime minister took control of the country and the king and queen returned to Bangkok.

When Elmer returned home he told me that he had been downtown when he saw tanks and army trucks filled with soldiers holding guns. It was back at the guest house that he found out that there had been a coup.

The *Bangkok Post* on September 10, 1985, stated, "There have been eight successful coups d'etat and another eight abortive ones including yesterday's incident."

In between coups, we coped with threats of invasion by the communists. Even as far back as 1953, radio broadcasts warned of possible invasion of Thailand by the communists. A letter I wrote to Mom provides some detail:

> *Things look bad here. The communists have invaded Laos and our radio reports say Thailand will be next. We might have to evacuate. We'll lose all of our belongings, but God will supply our needs. All we can do is keep working and praying. We live from day to day. When we came to Thailand in 1950, we did not know if we would be able to stay even a year because of the war in Korea. This part of the world was in great turmoil. Our chairman told us at the time, "Don't unpack all of your drums yet—just wait." But maybe the time has come when we'll have to leave. Only God knows what tomorrow holds.*

In the middle of 1953, Rev. Chrisman instructed us to pack immediately and leave Nongkai. The situation along the border was very tense with communist forces having advanced almost to the Mekong River on the Lao side.

Barbed wire fences were placed at both ends of our street because the Thai governor lived in the area. Bombing had been going on across the river all through 1952, but now the danger was very close. We packed. It was difficult not knowing what to take in view of the fact that we might never return. I packed documents, photo albums, keepsakes and clothing. Then we went to Bangkok.

When conditions improved, Elmer returned to check on things in Nongkai. I returned later on the train. Despite continued uncertainty, we settled into our home. The police ordered us to keep a 50-gallon drum of water in our front yard in case someone might try to burn the house of "the foreigners."

The March 11, 1967, issue of the *Bangkok Post* carried a special news report: "The United States government officially acknowledged yesterday for the first time that American planes based in Thailand are used in bombing North Vietnam." We had known for a long time about the bases and the bombing, but never wrote a word about this to anyone.

On April 10, 1975, I was in Bangkok attending a seminar. I wrote to Mom:

> *This is the place to be for up-to-date news of the Vietnam missionaries. All personnel are being sent out of Cambodia and Vietnam. Such stories we are hearing from the 25 or more missionaries here now in the Bangkok guest home. It all happened so fast. Most of them lost everything except what they could carry in a suitcase. There is no new word on our five captured missionaries. The Mission is seeking every way to have them released.*

Realizing my mother must be worrying about what might happen to us, on April 20, 1975, I wrote:

> *Things here in Thailand are under control. If it gets worse, we will leave. But do not look for us to return because so far we are free from trouble. Thank you for praying. We work while we are able to work. There is no new information on the five missing missionaries.*

On June 29, 1975, I saw an article in the Bangkok paper that made me feel very uneasy. It stated that on July 4th, American Independence Day, Thai students planned to turn out in strength to launch a new campaign. Their purpose was to secure the complete independence and sovereignty of Thailand. They would demand that all American soldiers be out of Thailand within one year.

We had always felt welcome in Thailand, but now there was a clear anti-American momentum gaining amongst the students. For the first time we saw "Yankee Go Home" posters. We decided that it would be wise to stay indoors on July 4th. We heard that a few students had set up tents in the center of Khon Kaen, but that the police had been able to maintain order.

On May 21, 1976, the prime minister of Thailand made a radio announcement: "All remaining United States military personnel

apart from 270 advisors have been asked to leave the country within four months."
Newspaper reports published the following day said that the announcement had been made following a deadlock in Thai-U.S. negotiations over American personnel stationed in Thailand.

On July 4th of that year (1976) we again saw the familiar "Yankee Go Home" slogans even though American equipment and buildings were being handed over to the Thai government. We personally experienced no hostility. The U.S. servicemen left. We had come before any of them and we stayed after they left.

One of the most thrilling experiences of my missionary career was to be at the Bangkok airport when our Vietnam missionaries who had been prisoners stepped off the plane from Hanoi. The High Commissioner for Refugees chartered a Royal Air Laos DC-3 plane to go to Hanoi to bring the 14 released prisoners back.

On October 31, 1975, at four p.m. I watched my dear friend, Betty Mitchell, step off the plane and greet her daughter, Geraldine, standing next to me. Dr. and Mrs. Richard Philips and Rev. and Mrs. Norman Johnson also arrived on that plane. The ambassadors of the United States and Canada as well as many United Nations officials were also there to greet them. Dr. Nathan Bailey, president of The Christian and Missionary Alliance, and Dr. Louis King, vice-president of Overseas

Ministries, were there to meet our missionaries.

Amid hugs, kisses, tears and flashing cameras, the new arrivals were taken to a VIP room inside the airport for a closed-door briefing before meeting the large group of reporters including those from major news magazines, television stations and local newspapers. Only people with passes were allowed in. Elmer, as chairman of the Mission, was permitted to go in. Being his wife, I was also allowed in. It was such an exciting experience to talk with our missionaries and to share in the joy of that wonderful occasion.

When Vietnam, Cambodia and Laos fell, many thought Thailand would be next. President Dwight Eisenhower in 1954 had used the expression "domino theory." He likened Indochina to a row of dominoes and said that the fall of any country in the region would threaten the stability of the entire area. As one country after another fell to the communists, it appeared that Thailand would be the next domino.

But Thailand has a reputation for being a survivor. The word "Thai" means "free." Thailand remained independent when her neighbors had been colonized. Even though problems at the borders continued to make headlines, Thailand did not become a domino. It developed its own style of democracy and presently is numbered among the most stable countries in the region.

We never did have to leave Thailand. God brought us through crisis after crisis. He helped us adjust to changing political situations and enabled us to cope with repeated threats of invasion. When we finally did leave Thailand, it was our own choice. We had finished our course.

16

On the Road Again

Dear Mom,
Last night we slept on the floor. Right
underneath us were two pigs who grunted
most of the night. Cows and buffalo also
moved around down there and bumped
the posts holding up the house. Quite a
place! That was our second night here. I
am afraid of the owner's dogs.

As soon as our last child went away to boarding school, I too became a "village missionary," and was no longer "the widow with a husband." I had waited about 18 years to be able to go with Elmer to the villages. Now we were both involved in extended teaching ministries, five-day evangelistic campaigns, 10-day Bible conferences and church growth seminars. We were often gone three weeks at a time. After a few days at home we would be off again.

The "village missionary" life took considerable adjustment on my part. In the villages I used the Thai country-style long skirts. Our notes had warned: "Ladies, special attention should be paid to safe skirt lengths and styles appropriate for ladder climbing and sitting on the floor in nationals' homes. It is better not to use slacks and pedal pushers in public. Don't wear shower slippers when teaching a class and don't dress too casually. Custom, not climate, is the criterion."

Finding appropriate sleeping arrangements was also a major problem. Even in the larger towns we sometimes had difficulty finding a suitable place to sleep. Although we liked to stay in old Chinese inns or small motels, there were not many alternatives. We had to take whatever we could find and most of the time that wasn't much.

In one large town, we stayed in three different hotels. I had names for each of them. "Knock on the Door Hotel" turned out to be an establishment that prostitutes frequented. After the first knock on our door, we decided to find another hotel.

"Broken Toilet Hotel" on our first visit looked new, but over the years repairs were never made and the place rapidly deteriorated. The "No Water Hotel" was a new, delightful, three-story hotel. However, we soon found out that the water did not reach the third floor! Buckets were carried up by the workers for our entire week there.

Most of our travels were to very small villages, so we slept with any Thai family that would invite us. It was disconcerting wondering day after day where our "home" would be that night. We took along sleeping bags, thin foam rubber mattresses, pillows and always mosquito nets. Many of the Thai homes were simple thatched-roof houses with no furniture. "I wonder where I'll sleep tonight" became my theme song.

I will always remember one experience I had in a small village. A Thai woman took us over to her newly built large wooden house. I thought, *This looks great!* We climbed the wooden stairs leading to the family's living quarters. Most Thai homes in the villages were built on huge posts supporting the house, with the chickens and pigs living in the open space underneath. Buffalos and cows also shared that space at night.

The woman took us to an open area in the center of the house—a room-sized hallway with doors all around leading into other rooms. She pointed to the floor in the hallway area and said, "Here is where you can sleep." I tried not to show my disappointment. I knew that the family members would have to pass through that area and I dreaded the lack of privacy. I wondered where we would hang our clothes and put our teaching materials.

Elmer asked our hostess if there wasn't a room somewhere else in the house that we could use. She said, "Yes, I have a small storeroom, but you would have to remove the rice sacks and clean the room." I was so happy to have some privacy that I gladly swept out the cobwebs, dirt and rice. Our hostess could not understand why these foreigners would choose a small room with one little window instead of a big open hallway with breezes!

One day, looking through an American magazine, I saw a picture of an A-frame folding travel trailer. *What a blessing that would be in the villages*, I thought.

On furlough, in 1967, we took the opportunity to look for such a trailer. We soon discovered that they were not easy to find. We had almost given up the search when I heard of an RV dealer only 10 miles from home. What a pleasant surprise to find that he had a folding trailer just like the one I had seen in the magazine! We knew it would be perfect for traveling in the villages.

"We'll be back," we told the dealer. "We want to take this to Thailand."

The salesman didn't know that we didn't have the money for the trailer, but we knew that if God wanted us to have it, He would provide the funds. We determined not to make any public appeals for this project, either by speaking or letter. Wanting to be sure this was God's will for us, I put out a fleece, asking Him for $500 to come in from a source outside of The Christian and Missionary Alliance.

I'll never forget the day this prayer was answered. A pastor friend of ours from an independent church came to visit. We were sitting in the kitchen drinking coffee when, without any mention of the trailer, he said, "How would you like $500 for something special for yourselves? It is not to go for any mission project. It must be for a personal need."

I almost fell off my chair! As we told him about the trailer and the fleece, we rejoiced together, knowing that God would send in the rest of the needed amount.

He did. We received not only sufficient funds for the trailer itself, but enough to cover the shipping and import duty.

Back on the field, I wrote to my mother:

> We have our trailer now and we sleep so much better. We even have a little privacy during the day. It stays snug and dry in heavy rainstorms and trails along so well behind our pickup even on the rough roads. You ought to see the faces of the people when we start cranking it up. The Thais say, "You are like the Apostle Paul—you bring your own tent." They also say, "You are no trouble now!"

The third adjustment I had to make to the itinerant lifestyle was eating Thai food at every meal. Thai food is very peppery hot and spicy and although Elmer always enjoyed hot food, I did not fare so well. The village people ate rice and fish two or three times a day. Sometimes a curry or soup with vegetables was also served. I never did get used to eating fish at breakfast time! I always took only a small portion of the hot food and diluted it with a lot of rice. The trailer proved a blessing here too—we could at least have an American breakfast.

Another sometimes traumatic adjustment I had to make was to the pot-holed, dirt roads. Many hours were spent bouncing in and over such roads. We rode in Land Rovers until 1973 when we purchased a Toyota lightweight pickup truck. The Mission doctor had warned us to be careful of what he called "Land Rover back," a common ailment among missionaries.

My journals contain many descriptions of these trips:

> *The roads were full of deep holes. I felt all battered when we arrived and still do. Because of heavy rains, one road was extremely slippery. I was ready to get out as a truck approached us sliding all over the road. We managed to stay on the road and avoid the truck, but we saw trouble ahead. A huge lumber truck, stuck fast in deep mud, was blocking five or six buses that didn't have enough room to go around. There was barely enough room on the narrow road for our small pickup to get around them all. One more hour and we would never have made it through the mud.*

I had the most difficult times coping with the numerous dilapidated or unfinished bridges we had to cross, especially in remote areas. Many times I told Elmer, "Let me out! I'm walking across!" One time, because we had guests, I refrained from my usual line. When we arrived at the meeting place, the leader told us, "You should not have gone on that bridge. I had planned to meet you there before you arrived." That really bolstered my confidence! On the return trip, even though the bridge was supposedly fixed, everyone except Elmer got out and walked across. A young Thai guided Elmer and the vehicle over the bridge because most of the new planks were not yet nailed down.

Another time, heavy rains had caused the approach to a long bridge to be washed out. A makeshift wooden bridge had been built starting at the bottom of the one bank and reaching to the other side. As we approached the bridge, I became very nervous. We started across. Thinking that at any moment we could slide right off into the river, my hand was on the door handle, ready to open it and jump into the swirling muddy river. We made it across, but the Land Rover could not get up the slippery bank. I got out and climbed up to the highway. Elmer hired 10 Thai men to help him push the vehicle up the bank to the main road.

I rehearsed the incident for our field newsletter:

On this last trip, I wish you could have seen the Sahlberg Land Rover slither, slide, spin and skid, slowly snaking up that slippery, slushy, soggy slope.

Traveling to the Thai villages wasn't all bad bridges and rough roads. In remote villages especially, there was a rather unique thing we had to get used to—being stared at. I remember particularly the first village I visited. Some older Thai women were not paying attention to the preacher, but were edging closer and closer to where I stood at the edge of the crowd. One old women finally reached out her hand and touched my ankle. Then she shouted some words in Thai. Later, I found out what she said: "Look at her skin. It stretches!" That was the last time I wore stockings in the villages!

For six years Elmer and I traveled together all over northeast Thailand. Often as many as 1,000 people attended the tent campaigns. In most areas the majority of the people had never heard about Jesus or knew Him only as an historical figure. We gave out thousands of tracts to help people understand the message.

Approximately 95 percent of the Thai people are Buddhist. We made it a practice never to speak against their national religion and warned our Thai Christians not to do so either.

During one meeting, however, a Thai preacher started to denounce Buddhism. We shuddered as a man from the congregation strode up to the front of the tent. He grabbed the microphone and shouted angrily, "You are a traitor to your country!" The crowd agreed with him. Elmer, sensing potential for possible violence, quickly dismissed the meeting.

Our trailer was parked by the side of the tent. I was very nervous that night, expecting any time to have rocks hit our roof or the trailer to be pushed over on its side. Thankfully, nothing happened. The next day Elmer went to the local authorities to explain our position. God intervened and we were allowed to continue with the services.

God intervened in a most unusual way on another occasion. One windy night in a Korat City campaign, the tent collapsed. We continued the meeting outdoors and prayed that the rains would hold off until it ended. Later on, we learned that it had rained in other parts of the city which circled our location. God had answered our prayers.

When Elmer became chairman of the Thailand Mission, we could not spend long periods of time in the villages. Inasmuch as clean and comfortable new motels and hotels were springing up in many areas, we decided that it was time to sell our little blue "home." There was also another reason for selling the trailer: we no longer felt safe in it because of increased communist activity and the growing crime rate. The villagers were also concerned for our safety and even posted an all night guard around us one night. That was the last time I ever slept in the trailer.

Throughout all our years of ministry in the villages, God kept His hand upon us. We were very happy in spite of the many unusual and primitive conditions under which we lived and ministered. We knew we were doing God's will.

17

Dumb like a Buffalo

In 1970, I was asked to speak at a United States servicemen's retreat in Thailand on the subject of the positions and attitudes of Thai women in a Buddhist society and the part of missionaries in changing the status of Thai women.

I researched the subject in every book and magazine I could find. I learned that indeed missionaries had had a large part in changing the status of Thai women. As early as 1865, missionary women started classes in their homes for Thai girls. At that time, only boys were being taught at the temples. One missionary, a Miss Cole, was asked to train women teachers for government schools. By 1900, all women teachers in the 13 government schools were graduates of that Mission school.

I also found reports stating that in past years Thai women believed that women were born to serve men. A famous Thai poet of the 18th century, Sun Thon, had written some instructions for women: (1) Walk slowly and don't talk; (2) When sleeping, don't turn over and disturb your husband; (3) Get up before your husband and prepare water for him to wash in; (4) When your husband is eating, sit nearby and watch him so that when he needs something, he doesn't have to shout; (5) Wait until he finishes eating before you eat.

Some of these rules were still being followed in the villages. In the cities, however, Thai women were demanding certain rights and recognition and many women were becoming leaders in business and professional fields. In the course of my research, I personally interviewed a Buddhist woman who was the manager of a bank.

Her Majesty, Queen Sirikit, worked tirelessly for the people of Thailand. The Thai women loved and respected her and she influenced their lives greatly, even to setting dress styles.

As we visited the village churches, I felt burdened for the women. They did not seem to be learning much at the regular services. The children distracted them and sometimes the teaching was too deep for them to grasp. I decided that the women needed their own meetings.

I approached Elmer about my desire to start women's meetings in the country areas. He presented the idea to the men of the churches. They did not want such meetings.

After considerable discussion, however, Elmer was able to persuade the men to allow some women's meetings on a trial basis. When he suggested that the men watch the children while I taught the women, we really ran into opposition! However, they eventually went along with that idea as well, and the women were able to enjoy their own meetings.

During the discussions in one village, a man stood up in a public meeting and told the entire congregation, "My wife is dumb like a buffalo. She can't learn!" His wife was sitting right there!

We went ahead anyway and held separate meetings for the women during the five-day campaign. At the joint meeting at the end of the conference, Elmer asked the men to stand and recite the books of the New Testament. The man with the "dumb" wife was not able to do it. The women were then asked to do the same. The "dumb" wife correctly named all the books! The only comment from her husband was, "She pronounced Second Thessalonians wrong!"

Very slowly, over the years, the village women learned the value of having their own meetings. At first, I did all the planning and teaching, but the time came when the women themselves assumed leadership and responsibility. They even made the decision to join together with other groups in the area. The women sent a letter inviting me to come to their first area meeting. We learned there that they had invited the head man of the county to open the meeting. No one really expected such an important person to attend a small village meeting of

Christian women, but right on time, the man walked in and opened the three-day seminar. I knew then that these village women could conduct their own meeting.

I was overjoyed when I heard that they wanted a central annual meeting where village women could join with the city women. That had been a dream of mine for 20 years. They had finally caught the vision.

Plans were made for the first All Northeast Women's Retreat. A Thai committee, with only one missionary advisor, organized the event to be held at the Central Bible School in Khon Kaen in 1982.

Two hundred women, ranging in age from 20 to 90, showed up! Each woman was given a color-coded name tag which determined the group's responsibility for work in the kitchen, in the bathroom (drawing water), cleaning the grounds and helping to keep the auditorium clean. Each group also presented a skit at the retreat.

Two professional male cooks took care of the meals. To my surprise, the husbands agreed to assume responsibility for the children at home so that their wives could attend the four-day conference. Only nursing mothers were allowed to bring children to the retreat.

A special feature of the first night's celebration was eating a huge cake, five and half feet long by two feet wide, trimmed with pink and white frosting. The speakers brought messages on family life, marriage and problems in the home. The women enjoyed the fellowship of small group devotions, congregational singing, special music and even a morning exercise hour. An afternoon break with games and shopping at the "Handicraft and Used Clothing Bazaar" provided fun for everyone. One elderly lady told me, "I haven't laughed so much in years. I forgot all my sorrows and troubles that I have at home."

I stood at the back of the large auditorium and viewed the proceedings. All over that room I saw women I had known for years. One of the leaders had been one of the shyest young country girls I had ever known.

My heart was singing as I returned home and I thanked God for allowing me to see a dream come true.

"Elmer," I said, "now I can retire happily. This part of my work is done. The Thai women are able to carry on the ministry."

And carry on they did! Each year the attendance at those retreats increased until 1987 when I heard that 700 women had attended. Fifty of them were non-Christians and 45 of them made a decision to accept Christ as their Savior.

The Thai women had proven they could learn and could conduct their own meetings. They were not "dumb like buffaloes!"

18

Hold Up Your Fingers

Dearest Mom,

We are living right in the middle of a leprosy colony—in our travel trailer, of course. Many of the people here have no fingers and many have only parts of feet. Some can hardly walk. Many faces are badly disfigured.

How thankful we should be for our strong healthy bodies. The Christians have a happy spirit in spite of their terrible disease and the lack of material things.

I remember so well the first leprous person I ever saw. I had been in Thailand about one month. As the woman walked toward me on a street in Korat City, I was shocked to see only a gaping hole where her nose should have been. Because of the estimated 150 to 200 thousand victims of leprosy in Thailand, The Christian and Missionary Alliance decided in 1950 to open a ministry among them. According to a government seminar paper, 60 percent of the leprosy cases were in the area in which we worked.

The Mission invited Dr. Richard Buker, an authority on leprosy, to come to our annual conference at the Central Bible School in Khon Kaen to teach us how to recognize and treat the disease. The American Leprosy Mission supplied the medicine, called DDS (a sulfone drug). Those pills, if taken over a long period of time, could arrest, but not cure, the disease. Recently, a new drug has been discovered that actually cures leprosy.

Leprosy, Dr. Buker told us, causes numbness in the extremities that often leads to accidental burning or mutilation. This is the source of the myth that leprosy causes parts of the body to fall off. Dr. Buker explained that leprous people do not feel pain, but they do suffer the same injuries as other people.

One cool night, my husband squatted with a group of Thai men around a sputtering camp fire. One of the men, who had leprosy, walked over to another fire. He started to pick up a red hot piece of wood.

"Don't pick that up!" someone cried. But he didn't listen. He was badly burned.

The leprosy bacillus was discovered in 1872 by a Norwegian doctor, Armauer Hansen. Leprosy, also called Hansen's disease, has an incubation period of three to five years or longer. It is not hereditary, but it does seem to run in families. Researchers are still not certain how the disease is transmitted. During our years in Thailand, we heard many different opinions—that the bacteria could be swallowed in food or dust, or that bugs or lice transmit the disease. All seemed to agree on one point—that bacteria could pass through broken skin.

We decided to be extra cautious. Our early orientation notes had warned: (1) Shoes, not open sandals, must be worn in leprosy clinics and centers. (2) Children of missionaries should not go into leprosy clinics or colonies. (3) Keep cuts and open wounds covered with bandages.

In July 1951, The Christian and Missionary Alliance opened its first leprosy clinic where medicine and the gospel could be given to the people. Many accepted Christ as their Savior. Additional clinics were started in various areas with such widespread response that preachers and teachers were needed for the many new believers. In May 1953, the Mission started the first Bible Training Institute for people with leprosy—Maranatha Bible School.

At one remote village, I taught 25 Christian women a course entitled, "How to Be a Witness." I held up my hand to illustrate how each finger represented one of the five points of my lesson. I asked the women to hold up their fingers as we went through the lesson. Suddenly, I realized that most of them did not have five fingers because they had leprosy.

Embarrassed, I turned to a black board behind me and drew five steps on the board and continued with the rest of the lesson. Never again did I use fingers to illustrate any lesson taught in those areas.

At another village we were holding a five-day Bible conference. The second day of the conference I taught the women about how God answers prayer. That very afternoon, a month-old baby started to cry. At first we thought it was a hunger cry, but we soon realized the child was in terrible pain. The father, a fine Christian, asked the church leaders to pray for the child, who by then was vomiting violently.

In addition to having leprosy, the father had lost his first wife, who was pregnant at the time, and a six-year-old son in a drowning accident, leaving him with three small children. He had remarried and now had this baby.

After prayer, the baby quieted down.

That night, the silence of the village was shattered once again by the screams of the baby. Soon the family arrived at my door and asked for medicine. I knew that medicine could endanger the life of such a young child, especially when the problem had not been diagnosed. If anything happened, I could be blamed.

I went into our camper and prayed that the Lord would give me wisdom. I took our emergency kit and gave the baby a drop of medicine. There seemed to be no adverse reaction. I held him in my arms for about two hours and he slept peacefully all the while. The situation seemingly under control, the parents took the baby and went home.

An hour later, the screams started again. Elmer and I lay in the dark praying and waiting.

"Please, dear Lord, do a miracle," I cried. "Heal this child. These people in this village need to see that our God lives, that He does answer prayer."

The screams increased in intensity and my heart ached for both the little one and his parents. I had just about decided to get up and go to help when the crying stopped as suddenly as it had begun. We listened for a long time. Only silence. God had answered prayer. He had touched the baby.

The following evening the unsaved mother accepted Christ as her Savior. Then together, the mother and father dedicated the baby to the Lord. The baby slept peacefully through the entire proceedings.

Seven years later, I met that little boy again. His mother came running over to our vehicle as we drove into the village.

"This is the baby you prayed for that night!" she beamed as she pointed to an obviously healthy child standing beside her.

In 1970, we spent a most memorable Easter in a very small leprosy village.

"No fancy church, no beautiful organ, no pretty new clothes here," I wrote to friends. In fact, there wasn't even a special Easter meal. But God honored the preaching of His Word and four people accepted Christ. What a marvelous, joyful Easter we spent away out in that isolated village even without the extras.

We obtained permission from authorities to take our folding trailer inside a government-sponsored leprosy colony. We wanted to live there while we held five days of meetings in their chapel. It was one of the strangest experiences of my life in Thailand.

The five days seemed like five weeks. But time mattered only to us. It did not matter to those people. They lived in their own circumscribed world—no newspapers, no radios, no television. I looked at the row upon row of little wooden houses in the colony and knew that each one housed at least one person who had leprosy. Men and women hobbled around, some on crutches and some on badly disfigured feet.

The Christians gathered at the chapel for the meetings. I'll never forget the sight of them singing the praises of God—praises and not complaints, in spite of ever-present rejection and suffering.

Years later, when it was time for us to return to America to retire, we stopped by the same colony for a farewell service. At that meeting, the leader asked if anyone wanted to say "special words" to the Sahlbergs who were returning to America.

One of the men stood to his feet. We had known him for many years. Elmer had worked with him in campaigns. He had learned to be a cobbler at our Bible School and now he made shoes for people with disfigured feet. His wife, a special friend of mine, had become a leader in women's work. She did not have leprosy.

Tong Sigh recounted this story.

> About 25 years ago, I was a student at the Maranatha Bible School for people with leprosy. Students who applied to the school had to state that they were Christians. I lied. I wanted to study there only to get a better education and to get treatment for my leprosy. I have never until now told you, Teacher Sahlberg, that you were the one who led me to find Jesus as my Savior. You came to the school to hold some meetings. I went to the altar, but I did not go to dedicate my life for service as you had asked. I went to receive Jesus as my Savior. That day I became a Christian. I want to thank you now.

At another meeting later that day, a young Thai girl came forward and presented us with a farewell gift from the church. Tears came to my eyes as she placed a small powder can containing Thai coins in my hands. Those people had given of the little money they had out of love and appreciation. I still have that little can. Sometimes when I speak, I show the can and tell how those leprous people expressed their love to God and to us. How little they had, but how thankful they were!

We did not realize how deeply the people felt about their deformities until one of them came to talk to Elmer after he had preached on the resurrection. Elmer had emphasized that in the resurrection we would have new bodies.

The man looked at Elmer's hands. Then he held out his own badly deformed hands.

"Someday in heaven, Teacher," he said looking up at Elmer with a smile, "I will have hands just like yours!"

19

Just Eat—Don't Ask

One question that all our visitors to Thailand, including many Alliance Youth Corps college students, asked was, "How do I get out of eating what I feel I just can't eat?" They did not wish to offend the Thai people, but their question was a valid one. Just what does one do when your stomach turns flipflops at the very thought (or sight) of something strange?

I always felt great empathy for the visitors, for I shall never forget asking myself exactly the same question on a certain occasion.

At breakfast one morning, our Thai hostess said, "I have a very special treat for you!" With that, she placed a dish full of fried silk worms in the center of the table!

Elmer and I, as honored guests, were seated at that very table. I had to think fast. As my stomach cartwheeled involuntarily, my eye caught sight of a group of women and children sitting on a mat nearby. Pointing to the group, I said, "Is that fish they are eating?"

The hostess replied, "Yes, would you like to

have some?" With that, she went to the kitchen and soon appeared with some "regular" fish. She was so anxious to please me that no one even noticed (I don't think) that I didn't eat the silk worms. Elmer did eat the "special treat." But then, he was used to eating strange things!

In response to the question about how to avoid eating certain foods, we usually told our visitors: "Just eat and don't ask." We knew that they would certainly not eat some of the "special" Thai food if they asked too many questions. Of course, we made sure that the food we encouraged them to eat would not make them sick.

In every Thai community, large or small, there were open-air marketplaces. Most Thai families did not own a refrigerator, so a daily trip to the marketplace was a necessity for them.

We always took our visitors to see the market, but it was usually *after* they had eaten at our house. We knew that they would consider the meat section of the markets especially uninviting. Huge chunks of beef and pork, brought in daily from the slaughter houses, hung from hooks over open counters. Pigs heads were displayed on tables, along with various slabs of fat, intestines and other "curious" cuts of meat.

We did our household shopping in the same markets. But personally, I thought it was better if I didn't see the meat section, or even smell it. And besides, our Thai helper knew how to bar-

gain much better than I did! She would get to
the market very early in the morning in order to
get the best of everything, especially the choice
cuts of meat.

Many other unusual things could be found in
those markets—dried beetles, toasted frogs,
lotus nuts, slabs of honeycomb, barbecued
chicken on a stick, eels in pails of dirty water,
fresh or smoked fish and dried squid—one of
our children's favorite snacks.

There were also piles of fresh red peppers
and crocks full of fermented fish sauce.
Authentic Thai food always includes those hot,
red peppers and that fish sauce. Counters over-
flowed with mangoes, papayas, onions, yams,
bananas, string beans and seasonal vegetables.
Baskets containing all kinds of food filled the
narrow aisles between the counters. Brown duck
eggs and white chicken eggs were stacked on
the floor. Large pans and all sizes of bowls
were filled with ready-made Thai curries and
various kinds of peppery sauces.

The basic customs and manners of the Thai
controlled every marketplace transaction.
Bargaining was an established way of life which
not only saved money—it also prevented cheat-
ing. But bargaining had strict rules: (1) Never
bargain unless you intend to buy; (2) If the
price you offer is accepted, you are obligated to
buy; and (3) Don't bargain too much. If you are
not satisfied, go to another store.

The markets also provided a place where

friends met, gossip was exchanged and romances were kindled. Thai women always dressed in their best finery when they went to the market.

Exchanging goods for cash was also an important function of the markets. In country areas especially, the people ate mostly rice and fish. Women got up early to catch fish in near-by streams or ponds. The men worked in the rice fields and sometimes the children hunted for leaves and plants to eat. They seldom had meat. It was too expensive. Even their own chickens were not eaten, but were sold for cash to buy other things.

Often, if we were staying in a Thai country home for three or four days, we would buy some beef or pork and vegetables to share with the family. It was a very special treat for them.

Usually only two meals a day were served, the first at nine or 10 in the morning and the second about five o'clock in the late afternoon. The meal was served on a mat on the floor. In the center of the mat were several small bowls of hot, spicy fish sauce and three or four round baskets of sticky rice (called *cow neow*) which we ate with our fingers. Rule #12 in our orientation notes stated, "When eating sticky rice, take a small handful from the basket, tear off a bite-sized piece, dip it into the meat or vegetable dish in the center of the table and place the rice in your mouth. Never bite off from a large piece and then dip that larger piece back into the center container."

During our first years in Thailand, we had to order staples and canned goods from Bangkok. But because of the high prices and the cost of shipping, we tried to buy as much as possible at the local market. I wrote to my sister:

> *I feel like Mother Hubbard here. My food closet is always bare. We eat almost entirely from the local market. Sometimes I dream of all the canned food in the USA. But we get along all right. Bangkok prices are double the price of your foods there. As prices go up in America, they go up here, too.*

Once in a while, when someone sent us money marked for a special treat, we ordered cold cereal. Corn Flakes was all that was available then. We called them Gold Flakes because of the exorbitant price.

Many changes have come to Thailand since those years. Now there are grocery stores and even American-style supermarkets in the larger cities and towns. Most staples can be obtained in these stores, though prices are still high, especially on imported goods.

We always had to be prepared for the unusual. I recall one experience that I shall always remember as The Toasted Python Episode. We parked our Land Rover beside a wooden chapel after a long and tiresome trip to reach a small village. Three Thai Christians ran over to welcome us. The leader, old Father See, pointed to a blazing fire in the distance and said, "Adjan (Teacher), we are sorry that our special meal for you isn't ready. Do you want to wait an hour or so or do you want to eat right now? We have sticky rice and fish that you can eat now."

I suspected immediately that they might be cooking something that would not appeal to me. That word "special," when associated with food, always worried me!

I asked, "What is the special treat?"

Father See answered, "Yesterday we caught a 10-foot python. We must pull the thick body slowly through the fire in order to toast each part. We have toasted only about half of it and it will take at least another hour, maybe longer."

"We'll take the rice and fish," I replied without hesitation.

"How do I get out of eating unpalatable foods?"

The answers are many and varied. But if worst comes to worst, I guess I would have to say, "Just eat—don't ask!"

20

I Gave You to God

Dear Mom,

By now you probably have had a phone call from Evelyn in Ohio telling you the unbelievable news! I myself can hardly believe it. Yesterday I received permission from the Mission to go to the United States for a one-month visit with you. I will not use Mission money and it will be my vacation time.

David arrived at our front door here in Udorn the other day. What a shock! We thought he was there in Florida! It was then he told us that I was to go to the States for Christmas and that the children would pay the plane fare! So tonight, Elmer and David will go to Bangkok to buy the ticket.

I will stay there with you, Mom, until after your birthday. We will telegram the exact arrival time.

You know how I hate to fly—even with Elmer. But since our furlough isn't due for another year, I felt I wanted to see you. This all seems like a dream! I can hardly believe I'll be there for Christmas. Keep calm! I'll see you soon.

Mother was 86 years old and although she did not have a serious health problem, David felt that she probably would not live for another year and a half till our next furlough. He urged me to go and be with her for Christmas. I'm so glad I went.

It was a joyous reunion at my mother's home in New Port Richey, Florida. But Mother was quick to let me know how she felt about my coming back from Thailand before our furlough was due.

"Why did you leave Thailand?" she asked. "I gave you to God and I am not taking you back now. You don't have to take care of me. God will take care of me." After I explained to her that I was going to return to Thailand in one month, she was happy about my coming home.

I learned that Mother had four prayer requests and, as she put it, "God will answer them in His time."

First, she did not want to die alone. Second, she didn't want a lot of pain. Third, she didn't want to die in bed, and fourth, she didn't want to go to a hospital.

I thought her third request was unusual and asked her about it.

"My sister died in bed," she responded. "I don't want to be found lying dead in my bed."

Mom and I had a wonderful month together. We visited relatives and special friends. I helped her wrap her Christmas gifts and put up the Christmas tree. On Christmas Eve, we sat together in her living room and enjoyed the beautiful Christmas programs on television. Three of our children came during the holidays and Elmer and David managed to get a Christmas phone call through to us from Thailand.

My mother delighted in hearing me speak in some of the local churches. She was so happy to have a missionary daughter. We enjoyed long talks. I took many pictures. Each day was precious.

On her birthday, I bought a huge cake and invited her friends to the celebration. The very next day, January 19, 1982, Mother stood at the back door of her little house and watched me get into a car that would take me to the airport and back to Thailand. The month had passed all too quickly.

In April, Mother made a tape recording and sent it to me:

So long and not goodbye
And God be with you till we meet again.
God bless you all and be with you,
Till we meet again.
If not on earth, we'll meet up yonder in
*   the Glory Land.*
Say "so long," not "goodbye."

Someday it is "good morning" up there.
Thank you, Jesus.
Amen.

Within four months, she was in heaven. With her passing, I lost my most faithful prayer warrior and best letter writer. My loss was surely heaven's gain. I did not return to the States for her funeral and I was especially thankful that Dale was with Mother when God took her home. I felt he represented me. After the funeral, Dale wrote us a most comforting letter: "[Grandma] handled the stroke with a touching courage and I admired her composure. 'Jesus' was the last word she ever said. The funeral was sad, but beautiful. She was free."

I was comforted in knowing that I was in Thailand where she wanted me to be. She could have said, "Please don't go back. I am old. Stay with me. I need you." Instead, she sent me back to Thailand with the words, "I gave you to God as a missionary and I'm not taking you back from that promise!"

Oh, yes—God answered all four of her requests!

21

A Seed Is Sown

Elmer, Adjan Suprom, and the children—five-year-old David and baby Evelyn—didn't seem to mind the bouncing around, but I did! Seven hours in a Land Rover, over dirt trails and shaky log bridges was more than I could take.

I had known that the trip would be rough, but I wanted to visit some of the villages before we left on furlough. Elmer had been traveling to these villages for four years while I taught in our small town and I wanted to see his ministry first-hand.

Life in the villages was difficult—no electricity, no bathrooms and no stores. Each night it was a wait-and-see game before we found out where we would spend the night. We would bathe in the river and sit on grass mats on the floor to eat. People would stare at the strange-looking foreign children with the "gold" hair.

We had an afternoon service. Many Thai children gathered to hear Adjan Suprom tell the story of Jesus. After the meeting, one little boy, about four years old, approached me.

"Please come over to my house and see my mother. She just had a new baby girl."

I followed the boy through some banana groves over to a small grass-roofed shelter. Inside, his mother was lying on a wooden plank bed covered by a thin Thai cloth. Underneath the bed was a low-burning charcoal fire. The Thai village women believe they will recover from childbirth quicker if they abide by this custom (even though it might be 95 degrees outside). I greeted the woman and we chatted briefly.

In the evening, men, women and children from the village came and squatted outside on the ground or on straw mats to watch our slide presentation about the death and resurrection of Christ. The projector was powered by kerosene. A large white cloth, strung up between trees, served as the screen. The seed was being sown.

One day, Elmer and I walked into a Christian bookroom in Udorn to visit the Perkinses. A small group was gathered in anticipation of the English language Bible class that was about to begin.

As we entered, a young man jumped up.

"I know you! I remember you!" he exclaimed.

Elmer and I looked at each other. This young man did not look at all familiar to either of us. We did not even live in Udorn, yet he was insisting that he had met us.

"You came to my village when I was a small

boy, about four years old. You showed slides on a big screen out in a field. I remember the picture of Jesus on the cross. I remember the foreign lady going home with me to see my mother who had just had a baby."

Then Monosuk added, "And I remember the man with the big nose!"

Elmer smiled. It seemed that reputation followed him wherever he went.

As Monosuk continued, my thoughts went back to that trip to his village. I remembered going to the little thatched shack to visit the Thai woman who had just given birth.

"You did not return to my village," said Monosuk, looking directly at me.

He was right. I had stopped traveling with the children because that trip had been so difficult—sickness, lack of food and almost unbearable roads. But Elmer had not returned either. He had so many other villages to visit that he had not been able to go back.

Monosuk continued.

"My parents sent me to Udorn to become a teacher. A professor at the college told me I needed to learn English and advised me to go to a book room where some missionaries taught English. When I arrived, I saw a large picture on the wall—the picture of Jesus on a cross. It was the same picture I had seen in my village when I was a little boy. I accepted Jesus as my Savior after studying here with Mr. and Mrs. Perkins."

Monosuk became a leader in Campus Crusade for Christ in Bangkok. His father and mother and brother and sister all became Christians. His sister's conversion was particularly interesting to us. One day, after we had taught a Bible class, a young teenage girl came to accept Christ as her Savior. She was the baby I had visited so many years earlier!

A seed had been sown. Years later, it bore abundant fruit.

A little Thai boy named Teerawat attended children's meetings taught by George and Edna Heckendorf in the city of Kalasin. Even at an early age this little boy wanted to become a doctor, and for good reason. His father had been accidently shot by a hunter and did not receive medical care in time to save his life. The incident so motivated Teerawat that he enrolled in a medical school in Chiengmai in the northern part of Thailand. There the seed that had been planted in his heart as a child sprouted into life. Through the witness of a Thai doctor and the influence of Dr. Garland Bare, Teerawat Runpsaitong became a Christian.

Elmer and I met Dr. Teerawat in 1970 in a church service in Khon Kaen. He had driven over from Kalasin where he was working in a government hospital. As we talked together he shared a dream with us—a dream of having his own private hospital that would meet not only the physical needs of people, but also their spiritual needs. We encouraged him in that dream.

Dr. Teerawat began with a small, two-room clinic. Right from the start he made it known that he was a Christian. A large picture of Jesus hung in the waiting area and Christian literature was piled on the tables.

Dr. Teerawat moved from there to set up a 20-bed hospital right in the middle of a long, wooden, two-story building containing many little shops. Waiting rooms, offices and treatment rooms were on the first floor. The beds, on the second floor, were seldom empty.

In 1983, Dr. Teerawat's full dream became a reality. What a celebration there was for the opening of the only Christian hospital in northeast Thailand. The mayor of Kalasin was there. The governor of the province cut the ribbon and unlocked the door, officially opening a three-story, 100-bed facility. Elmer conducted the service of dedication before 300 guests. The Christian witness was obvious to all who toured the building—wall pictures of Jesus, video tapes of Bible stories on the television screen in the lobby, Christian literature displayed in conspicuous places and sacred music coming through the speakers.

Elmer and I rejoiced with Dr. Teerawat and his wife. Through the years, they and their four children had become a part of our family. It was through the influence of Dr. Teerawat that our daughter Esther went to medical school and became a surgeon's assistant.

Seeds were sown, sometimes with tears, sometimes with misgivings, sometimes wondering if they would ever take root. What a blessing it is to see the fruit of those seeds in the lives of people like Monosuk and Teerawat Runpsaitong.

> *He who goes out weeping,*
>   *carrying seed to sow,*
> *will return with songs of joy,*
>   *carrying sheaves with him.*
>
> *(Psalm 126:6)*

> *But the one who received the seed that fell on good soil is the man who hears the word and understands it. He produces a crop, yielding a hundred, sixty or thirty times what was sown.   (Matthew 13:23)*

22

We're the Team!

Team effort. That's what missionary work is all about. I have already shared with you how God in His great mercy and love saved Elmer and me and called us into His service and eventually to Thailand. Our testimonies, parts of which you read here, confirm the Scripture which says that we are laborers together with God. We were not alone in Thailand. God was there. We felt His presence. We saw the results of His power and intervention. More and more we realize what a privilege it was to be partners with Him in His worldwide missionary program.

But the teamwork reached into other areas as well. During our 35 years of ministry as husband and wife, Elmer and I always saw ourselves as a team. Prior chapters have described our partnership as "city missionary" and "country missionary" and the ways in which God helped us to cope with the situations that our lifestyle occasioned. There were times, I have to admit, when our team relationship created problems for me.

For instance, when Elmer became chairman of the Mission, life changed drastically for me. Because of his responsibilities, he often had to make decisions and solve problems in which I could have no part. I had been used to being his confidante. Now that was sometimes no longer possible. It was not easy for me to adjust to not being a team in that way. I often felt alone and uncomfortable.

Other problems arose as well when it became apparent that one of my ministries as part of the "chairman team" was to be hostess to Thai and American officials, Thai and Chinese business and professional people and various Mission leaders. I wrote to my mother:

> I must get used to having a lot of company. We have people staying with us every week for overnight or longer. Missionaries travel through or we keep special speakers for meetings in the city. I suppose I'll adjust to all this, but it is a strange new lifestyle for me after being alone so many years. I must also be careful to never express a strong opinion. I am supposed to take a middle view and see both sides of any issue or problem.

I tried as a member of the team to please everyone and be the "perfect" chairman's wife. But I soon learned that I could not please everyone. God used an article in a magazine to show me the futility of wearing myself to a frazzle trying to impress or be accepted by people. I finally came to realize that God knows, forgives, loves and accepts me as I am. I began to relax and enjoy my role. Although Elmer held the chairman's position for several different periods during our years in Thailand, I learned to fit into the demands of the position and not to be frustrated by them.

Team work? Oh, yes. Elmer and I were a team. God had led us together as husband and wife and called us to serve Him together. We were God's team.

Our teamwork also involved us with the refugees who were fleeing into Thailand from Laos, Cambodia and Vietnam. That ministry involved teamwork with Thai officials and United Nations representatives who met monthly to coordinate refugee projects.

We visited the first make-shift refugee camp that was set up on the Cambodian border when the military situation in Southeast Asia deteriorated. John and Jean Ellison worked at that camp. As the Ellisons translated for us, former army officers told how they had escaped from Pol Pot's regime, sometimes hiding for days in rice fields and jungles on their way to the border. Many told stories of the mass killing of the educated class. In their desperation, these people—teachers, nurses, doctors, army personnel—often pretended to be peasant farmers in order to escape the murderous rampage.

CAMA Services (the relief arm of The Christian and Missionary Alliance whose motto is "Turning Relief into Belief") eventually arrived to take over our work in the refugee camps. CAMA Services continues to this day to provide the basic necessities for life and living to refugees throughout Southeast Asia and other parts of the world.

I'll never forget the day when Wayne and Minnie Persons took us to an early Sunday morning worship service at a camp in Loei. Nine hundred people were seated on low, wooden, backless benches in a long, dirt-floored shelter. The grass roof was held up by bamboo poles. A second meeting later that morning saw another 900 or more gather to hear God's Word preached.

Team work? Oh, yes. It took a team to minister to those thousands of displaced persons. And God honored that effort.

The Sahlberg team, as you already know, eventually numbered four others with the same last name! We always included the children in our team. They helped to open doors of opportunity, especially in Nongkai province during our first years in Thailand. Many Vietnamese refugees had fled there during the Indochina War. The refugees blamed the Americans for helping the French government in that conflict. Only when the children were with me did I feel any friendliness on the part of the Vietnamese.

Being part of the Sahlberg team meant a different lifestyle for our children. In Thailand, David and Dale often traveled with Elmer to the villages. They sang, played the guitar and helped to set up the tent.

Furlough time had its own set of adjustments. Grandparents, aunts, uncles and cousins were all strangers to the children. They not only had to adjust to new relatives, but they had to make new friends as well. The one constant in all the newness was that our team of six was together. That was important.

As we traveled, the children took part in missionary meetings by helping in the skits, dressing in Thai clothes and singing in the Thai language. It was difficult for the children to stay in many different homes and live out of suitcases for weeks at a time.

They also had to adjust to calling many different places home. Because of Elmer's responsibilities, we moved 12 times in Thailand, not to mention the various homes we had while on furlough. Dale once asked, "Where is home?" It seemed we were forever packing. We even helped other missionaries pack and called ourselves The Sahlberg Packing Company.

Team work? Oh, yes. The Sahlberg family was a team.

Other key players on our team were the people who worked for us—the servants we called helpers. Coming from a land (America) where servants are a luxury, we sometimes felt uncomfortable with hired help. But we soon came to realize that they could free up our time for God's work. The low wages made it possible.

There were many ways our Thai helpers assisted us. In the early days, all the cooking was done on charcoal stoves. Later, with kerosene stoves, I was always nervous (with good reason) because of their unpredicability. Even our refrigerator ran on kerosene. In addition, water had to be drawn in buckets from a well on the property. It was many years before we got city water and over 20 years before we got hot water heaters.

During our years in Nongkai, clothes were scrubbed by hand on a little wooden platform in the back yard. They were ironed with charcoal irons. Our clothes often had little burn holes caused by sparks from the charcoal.

Having Thai helpers taught me that teamwork sometimes requires a lot of patience and effort. Teaching a Thai girl or boy to prepare food American-style demanded much time and energy. My instructions were not always clearly understood. It was often frustrating. After I had taught one girl how to make a coffee cake (or thought I had), I asked her to prepare one for some guests. The cake looked lovely as it came out of the oven. I cut a small corner piece and popped it into my mouth. Something was wrong. It had a strange, bitter taste.

"What did you put in the batter?" I asked the girl.

"Well," she said, "I ran out of flour, so I put in three-fourths cup of powdered coffee! You told me to make a coffee cake!"

No one could eat the cake. Even the dog refused!

In 1952, I wrote in my journal:

> *I once thought it would be so nice to have hired help but now sometimes I think it would be easier to do things myself. So many of my good things have been ruined. I must learn not to place such value on material things—even favorite, American treasures. And I need much more patience to live out here. We have to check to see that our dishes are properly washed and that our drinking water is boiled. If I had some modern conveniences, it would be easier to do the work myself. But it would be too much for me to go to the early morning market. We cannot afford canned goods, so daily trips to the local fresh food stalls must be made. And I would never keep up with the dust from the unpaved streets that blows in through our glassless windows.*

It was very annoying when trained members of our team left us for the higher wages offered by American soldiers or wealthy business people. As missionaries we could not match those salaries. Just when I had finally been able to get someone to cook the way we liked, she or he left and I had to start all over.

We had many wonderful helpers during our years in Thailand. They were truly helpers—not servants. They were part of our team. The ones who were Christians felt they were assisting us to do God's work. Some left us to enter full-time Christian ministry. Some were with us for over 10 years.

Team work? Oh, yes. Without our Thai helpers, we could not have accomplished what God wanted us to do in Thailand.

Elmer and I also worked in partnership with The Christian and Missionary Alliance national churches, called The Gospel Church of Thailand. Local churches invited us for ministry and we went at their request. We often teamed up with students from the Central Bible School in Khon Kaen who sang at our special meetings and tent campaigns. Christian teachers helped us in day ministries, along with Thai pastors and evangelists.

Adjun (teacher) Khum Jun, a Thai evangelist, often traveled with us or rode his motorcycle to meet us for special meetings in village churches. The three of us took turns speaking during the all-day and evening meetings. This faithful servant of God devoted his full time to evangelism, trusting Him to supply the needs of his family.

Team work? Oh, yes. Adjun Khum Jun and many others like him were part of our team.

A most necessary member of our team, we soon found out, was the Thai government, for we needed the visas and work permits that they could provide. As foreigners, we were very aware of how government regulations affected our lives. A constant companion everywhere we went was a little book called a police book (dong dao). That book was proof that we possessed a quota number.

A quota number is a permanent visa—a difficult document to obtain. It is valid as long as a person does not leave Thailand for longer than one year. Foreigners without a quota number must enter Thailand on a non-immigrant visa and then apply for an extended visa. Such a person, with non-immigrant status, could be summoned at any moment to appear within 48 hours at the immigration office in Bangkok. If he or she did not appear, or if the application was refused, that person would have to leave Thailand for brief periods once or even twice a year.

As you can imagine, much time and expense could be involved if one was unfortunate enough to be found in that situation. So, having a quota number was a top priority for us.

Because three of our children were born in Thailand and were therefore considered to be Thai citizens, they did not get a quota number. Instead, they carried American passports. That meant that they sometimes had to leave the country and re-enter to obtain visa extensions.

On January 26, 1965, I wrote my mother:

> *I have really been on the go. I had to take Esther out of the country [to Laos] because of a mix-up in her visa. David went along with us. Elmer stayed home with Dale. It took me two days to rest up after one week of traveling from one end of Thailand to the other by train, bus, ferry, station wagon and taxi. First, I had to go to the immigration department in Bangkok from our home in Korat—five hours on the train. Then, from Bangkok, another train ride up to the border. Thirteen hours on that train. We crossed the Mekong River to Laos on a ferry and enjoyed a brief visit with some missionaries and returned to Nongkai to ride the train back to Korat. Then back to Bangkok once again to the immigration office [with proof of our having exited the country].*

Elmer, David and I got our permanent quota numbers in 1950. In 1973, when a problem caused me to stay in America over the one-year limit, I lost my number. So, from 1973 on, I never knew when I would be asked to leave the country. It was difficult to plan meetings and classes (or anything else for that matter) with the 48-hour notice regulation hanging over my head.

For two and a half long years I kept applying for one of the 100 quota numbers that were allocated to Americans. What a happy day it was when it finally arrived. Could you guess what number it was? It was number 99!

The visa situation changed for the better when the Evangelical Fellowship of Thailand, composed of many evangelical missions, including our own, received official recognition by the Thai government.

Amidst the often prolonged frustrations of bureaucratic rules and regulations, once in a while a little serendipity relieved the tension.

One day, Elmer went to the Department of Education to see if the Alliance could set up the Dalat missionary school in Bangkok. The department's director general was not in, so Elmer asked to see his assistant. What a pleasant surprise to find out that the assistant was the woman who had taught me Thai in Korat many years earlier! She provided valuable information about how to organize the school and she became an important link in dealing with the complex government regulations.

Team work? Oh, yes. Sometimes working with government officials and adapting ourselves to their rules and regulations was frustrating and unpredictable. But it was teamwork nonetheless.

Every furlough we formed another team—a partnership with the Christians and churches in America. It was a significant and important relationship for many reasons, not the least of which being that every four years we had to cope with the problem of finding a house to rent.

On our 1961 furlough, Elmer and I searched day after long day for a place to live. The answer was always, "Sorry, no children. No pets." Besides, the rents were higher than we could afford to pay. Every day we returned to my mother's overpopulated little house wondering if we would ever get settled. Finally, after days of rejection and discouragement, we were able to find a new, three-bedroom house at the right price. It provided an enjoyable place to call home for a year.

As our next furlough (1967) drew near, hoping to avoid the house-hunting trauma of the previous furlough, we wrote to the pastor of the Largo (Florida) Alliance Church to seek his help. What an encouraging response we received from Pastor Arnold Johnson, his wife Mary, and their entire congregation. They found and rented a lovely house for us in an area close to schools, stores, the church and even to the beach. The women of the church cleaned the house until it sparkled. The congregation furnished it under a plan called "Loaned for a Year." There was even a piano for our daughter and a beautiful stone fireplace complete with a one year's supply of wood.

I'll never forget how happy I felt as I stepped into that lovingly prepared, beautiful home.

Those people, from the Largo Alliance Church, knew what teamwork meant.

It wasn't until 1972 (after 22 years of missionary service) that we knew for the first time where we would live during furlough. Through the generosity of my mother, we were able to purchase some land and place a repossessed mobile home on it. It was a wonderful feeling to finally have roots!

Finding good schools for the children took second place only to finding a home. Then, with the children enrolled in their respective schools, there was the matter of notifying relatives, friends and business offices of our new address. Finding a doctor and dentist was the next priority. We all had to have complete physicals.

Within weeks of arriving home, Elmer would begin to prepare for the fall missionary tour which usually lasted about 10 weeks. In The Christian and Missionary Alliance, wives are not asked to serve on a regular tour until the children have completed high school. We had four children born almost four years apart. That meant I had one child at home until I was almost ready to retire! It was not until 1983 that I was finally able to accept a tour assignment.

Preparing for tour meant writing a biographical sketch, getting a new photograph and preparing an assortment of messages and slide presentations. And, of course, there was the furlough ministries seminar, sponsored by the national office, which hopefully got the missionaries in step with the cultural and religious scene in America before sending them out to minister in the churches.

Home with the children, I had to start planning for the next five-(and later four-) year term. In the early days, suitable clothing, shoes and linens were not available in Thailand. That meant that I had to estimate sizes for four children for five years! It was no easy task.

We also had to provide towels, sheets, pillowcases and blankets for each child to take to boarding school. I spent hours and hours shopping for all these items. But buying them was only the beginning. After that, every towel, sheet, pillowcase, blanket and sock (for four years for four children!) had to have name tags sewed on!

My mother was always amazed at the piles of clothes, linens and small kitchen articles that accumulated in the garage every furlough. Before being packed into steel drums, each item was listed and priced for customs purposes. In Thailand, those drums in our storage room became my Five and Dime Store. As I periodically removed various articles, I thought of the women of the Women's Missionary Prayer Fellowships in the United States who were working together with us by supplying those necessities. Each trip to the barrels was a reminder of their love and dedication.

Team work? Oh, yes. One missionary family

home on furlough and hundreds of loving Christian people bountifully providing our needs. What a blessing! What a team!

Probably the most important team was the prayer team. As we ministered in Thailand, we counted on our prayer team at home. I remember writing to one prayer partner: "Sometimes we feel prayer as a cloak around us. It helps to know you are standing with us in prayer."

People have told me that they prayed for us every day. Whenever we faced some dangerous situation or some difficult experience, such as some I have shared with you, I would recall the names and faces of individuals who had assured me of their daily prayers for us.

Elmer wrote an article for the *Alliance Witness* of August, 1973: "A measure of success for our ministry has always been coupled with the prayer backing of people who are specific in their petitions for us." Only God knows what influence each person had through prayer in our ministry in Thailand.

One furlough, I noticed that a television channel in Florida began their evening news with a picture of four people exclaiming, "We're the team!" Then each one—the news reporter, the photographer, the sports announcer and the weatherman—were introduced to the audience. The next picture once again showed them, shoulder to shoulder, shouting, "We're the team!"

We, too, have been part of a team for 35

years. Hundreds of people have stood shoulder to shoulder with us: professors and pastors and a host of believers at home and abroad, fellow missionaries, national Christians, teachers and staff at our missionary school, fellow workers in literature, radio and evangelism ministries and many others too numerous to mention.

If you were part of that team, we thank you. If you were not, it is not too late to join the team. According to a May 1991 report, The Christian and Missionary Alliance has 1,246 licensed personnel serving in 38 countries of the world. Alliance-related ministries are carried on in an additional 16 countries, making a total of 54 countries in which The Christian and Missionary Alliance is represented.

Even though Elmer and I are retired, we are part of their team.

You can be part of their team, too.

We together are the team!

Epilogue

Corrine and Elmer Sahlberg retired in 1985 after 35 years of ministry in Thailand.

Corrine is happy in her ministries in the local church and speaking to various groups. Elmer returns to Thailand each year as an advance man to organize a program sponsored by Dr. Thomas Flynn, a neurosurgeon from Louisiana.

The team, which includes the Sahlberg's daughter, Esther, donates its time and talents for one month each year to work in Thai hospitals, performing brain and spinal surgery. After the medical team leaves, Elmer stays to visit Thai believers and to minister in the national churches.

Please Leave Your Shoes at the Door is the fifth book in a continuing collection of missionary biographies. For more information on ordering other titles in the *Jaffray Collection of Missionary Portraits* contact your local Christian bookstore, or call Christian Publications toll-free **1-800-233-4443**. Ask to be put on the *Jaffray Collection of Missionary Portraits* mailing list. Then you will receive information when new titles are available.

Titles available as of Spring 1992:

Let My People Go
A.W. Tozer

"Weak Thing" in Moni Land
William Cutts

On Call
David Thompson

To China and Back
Anthony Bollback

Please Leave Your Shoes at the Door
Corrine Sahlberg

A Heart for Imbabura
Charles Shepson